The
Misspeller's Dictionary

Foreword

For years, good spelling has been equated with intelligence, when, in fact, there isn't the remotest relationship between the two. The way one spells most often depends on how one hears sounds or combinations of sounds.

The Misspeller's Dictionary is designed for the thousands of people who spell the way they hear. We began by compiling the most comprehensive list of words that are difficult to spell, and then we misspelled these words. One exception to our rule is that we did not misspell a word if a particular misspelling fell fairly close in alphabetical order to the actual spelling. If you can come that close to the correct spelling, you will be able to find it.

We did, however, misspell extremely difficult words like hemorrhoid (hemroid) because the misspelling very often did not look or sound like the actual word. We did not misspell every word, but we left the difficult words in so that you can check yourself when you get stuck.

The way to use this book is to look up the word you are trying to spell by the way it sounds to you. If the word you are looking up is printed in red type, you have misspelled it. The correct spelling of the word is in black, immediately adjacent to the red word. If the word is in black you have spelled it correctly. All correctly or incorrectly spelled words fall in the alphabetic master list on the left column. To help you with your spelling we have included some basic rules that you should read over and try to keep in mind.

Basic Rules of Spelling

Probably the toughest things to learn in spelling English words are the exceptions. Usually there is quite a list of them following every rule. The best thing to do is to memorize the rules and as many of the exceptions as possible. After awhile you may not remember the specific rule, but you won't forget the problem words.

First Rule
Adding a Suffix to One Syllable Words

Take the word "stop." It's a one syllable word ending in a single consonant (P), and the consonant is preceded by a single vowel (O). When adding a suffix. the last consonant is doubled:

    stop + ing = stopping
    hot + est = hottest
    big + er = bigger

However, the rule does not apply if a word ends with two consonants or if it ends with one consonant preceded by two vowels:

    stick + er = sticker
    sweet + er = sweeter

Second Rule
Adding a Suffix to a Word with Two or More Syllables

If a word is accented on the last syllable, treat it as if it were a one-syllable word. Double the last consonant if the word ends in a single consonant preceded by a single vowel.

prefer + ing = preferring

Again, the suffix must begin with a vowel.

If the word ends with two consonants or if the final consonant is preceded by two vowels, the rule does not apply.

If the word is not accented on the last syllable, just add the suffix.

The exception is simple. When the accent shifts to the first syllable of the word after the suffix is added, don't double the consonant. A dictionary will help you make the decision here.

Third Rule
Words Ending in a Silent *E*

Usually when the word ends with a silent *e*, drop the *e* if the suffix begins with a vowel:

glide + ing = gliding

Here the exceptions are many.

1. Words with a soft *g* or *c* sound keep the *e* if the suffixes *able* or *ous* are being added.

2. Again, keep the *e* if the word could be mistaken for another word:

dyeing, shoeing

3. If the word ends in *ie*, drop the *e* and change the *i* to *y* before adding *ing*:

dying, lying

4. When adding the suffix *age* to mile, line, acre, the *e* is not dropped.

Fourth Rule
Adding a Suffix with a Consonant to a Word with a Silent *E*

When adding a suffix that begins with a consonant, *ment, ness, less,* and so on, and the word ends with a silent *e*, usually keep the *e*. Some exceptions are judge, true, argue, whole, nine, acknowledge, and awe.

Fifth Rule
The *IE* and *EI*

Almost always use *i* before *e* except after *c*, or when the sound is *a*, like in neighbor and weigh.
The exceptions are:

ancient	neither
foreign	seize
Fahrenheit	sleight
forfeit	sovereign
height	surfeit
leisure	weird

Sixth Rule
Words Ending with *Y*

When a word ends with *y* and is preceded by a consonant, change the *y* to *i* and add the suffix.
Some exceptions are babyhood, beauteous, ladylike, plenteous, and wryly.
If the *y* is preceded by a vowel, there is no change.

A

abace	abase	aberigeny	aborigine
abacus		aberrant	
abait	abate	abet	
abase		abey	abbey
abate		abeyance	
abayance	abeyance	abhor	
abbacus	abacus	abide	
abbé (cleric, see abbey)		ability	
		abismel	abysmal
abberent	aberrant	abiss	abyss
abberigine	aborigine	abject	
abbey (church, see abbé)		ablate	oblate
		abliterate	obliterate
abbreviate		ablivious	oblivious
abbrogate	abrogate	abnormal	
abbrupt	abrupt	A-bomb	
abcense	absence	abominable	
abcent	absent	abomnable	abominable
abcess	abscess	abord	aboard
abdacate	abdicate	abore	abhor
abdamin	abdomen	aborigine	
abdicate		abortion	
abdomen		abragate	abrogate
abdominal		abrasion	
abduct		abreveate	abbreviate
abecus	abacus	abridge	
aberent	aberrant	abrogate	

abrupt
absalute   absolute
abscence   absence
abscent   absent
abscess
abscond
absence
absent
absess   abscess
absolute
absolve
absorb
abstain
abstinence
abstruse
absurd
abuse
abut
abysmal
abyss
academic
academy
a capella
accalade   accolade
accolite   acolyte
accede (agree,
   see exceed)
accelerate
accent
accept (receive,
   see except)
access (approach,
   see excess)
accessory
accident (miscue,

   see occident)
acclaim
acclamation
   (approval)
acclimation
   (adjustment)
accolade
accolite   acolyte
accommodate
accompany
accomplice
accomplish
accord
accordion
accost
account
accountant
accredit
accrete
accrimonious   acrimonious
accrobat   acrobat
accross   across
accrue
accumen   acumen
accumulate
accupuncture   acupuncture
accurate
accuse
accustom
acedemic   academic
acension   ascension
aceptic   aseptic
acetate
acetic (sour,
   see ascetic)

acetone		acrete	accrete
acetylene		acrid	
ache		acrimonious	
achieve		acrobat	
Achilles'		across	
tendon		acru	ecru
Acilles'	Achilles'	acrue	accrue
tendon	tendon	acsent	accent
	acetate	acsesory	accessory
acknowledge		activate	
aclaim	acclaim	activities	
aclair	éclair	actual	
acne		actuary	
acnowledge	acknowledge	acuity	
acolade	accolade	acumalate	accumulate
acolyte		acumen	
acomodate	accommodate	acumulate	accumulate
acompany	accompany	acupuncture	
acomplice	accomplice	acurate	accurate
acomplish	accomplish	acuse	accuse
acord	accord	acustics	acoustics
acordian	accordion	acustom	accustom
acost	accost	adage	
acount	account	adagio	
acountant	accountant	adamant	
acoustics		adanoid	adenoid
acquaint		adapt	
acquaintance		adaquate	adequate
acquiesce		addage	adage
acquire		addament	adament
acquisition		addative	additive
acquit		addendum	
acquittal		addenoid	adenoid
acre		addict	
acredit	accredit	additive	

address		adroit	
adduce		aduce	adduce
adegio	adagio	adue	adieu
adelescent	adolescent	adulation	
adelveiss	edelweiss	ad valorem	
adendum	addendum	advantageous	
adenoid		adversary	
adequate		advertisement	
adhere		advice	
adhesive		(suggestion)	
ad hoc		advise	
adict	addict	(give advice)	
adieu (good-bye,		advisable	
see ado)		adviser	
ad infinitum		Aegean	
adjacent		aegis	
adjective		aerate	
adjoining		aerial	
adjourn		aerie (nest,	
adjudicate		see airy)	
adjutant		aerodynamics	
ad-lib		aeronautics	
administer		aerosol	
administrate		aesthetics/	
admirable		esthetics	
admiral		afadavit	affidavit
admissible		afection	affection
ad nauseam		affable	
ado (trouble,		affadavit	affidavit
see adieu)		affect (influence,	
adobe		see effect)	
adnoid	adenoid	affidavit	
adolescent		affiliate	
adopt		affinity	
adrenal		affirmative	

afflict		agrarian	
affluent		agregious	egregious
afford		agression	aggression
affray		agriculture	
afghan		agrieved	aggrieved
afidavit	affidavit	agronomy	
afiliate	affiliate	ahlms	alms
afinity	affinity	ail (pain, see	
afirm	affirm	ale)	
afirmation	affirmation	air (oxygen,	
aflict	afflict	see err, heir)	
afluent	affluent	airy (open, see	
aforesaid		aerie)	
aforism	aphorism	aisle (passage-	
afraid		way, see I'll,	
afray	affray	isle)	
Afro		ajacent	adjacent
afrodisiac	aphrodisiac	ajatent	adjutant
agast	aghast	ajoining	adjoining
Agean	Aegean	ajourn	adjourn
agenda		ajudicate	adjudicate
agglomerate		ajutant	adjutant
aggrandizement		aknalege	acknowledge
aggravate		a la carte	
aggregate		alacrity	
aggressive		a la mode	
aggrieved		alamony	alimony
aghast		alan	elan/élan
agile		albatross	
agit	agate	albeit	
agitate		albetross	albatross
agnostic		albino	
agonize		albumen	
agrandizement	aggrandize-	Albuquerque	
	ment	alchemy	

alcohol		alligator	
ale (beer, see		allimentary	alimentary
ail)		allimony	alimony
alegation	allegation	alliteration	
alege	allege	allocate	
aleviate	alleviate	allot (assign,	
algae		see a lot)	
alias		allotment	
alibi		allowance	
alien		allowed (per-	
aligarchy	oligarchy	mitted, see	
align/aline		aloud)	
alimentary		alloy	
alimony		allready	already
aline/align		allude (refer to,	
aliteration	alliteration	see elude)	
alkali		all right	
all (the whole,		allure	
see awl)		allusion	
allay (relieve,		(suggestion,	
see alley,		see illusion)	
ally)		alluvial	
allbeit	albeit	ally (friend, see	
alledge	allege	allay, alley)	
allegation		almanac	
allege		almond	
allegiance		almost	
allegory		alms	
allergy		aloha	
alleviate		a lot (many,	
alley (passage,		see allot)	
see allay, ally)		alotment	allotment
alliance		aloud (out loud,	
allibi	alibi	see allowed)	
allien	alien	alpaca	

alphabet		ambulatory	
already		ameba/amoeba	
alright	all right	ameliorate	
altar (raised		amenable	
place)		amend	
alter (change)		(improve, see	
altercation		emend)	
alter ego		amenity	
alterior	ulterior	amertize	amortize
alternate		amethyst	
although		ametory	amatory
altimeter		amety	amity
altitude		amfedamine	amphetamine
altruism		amfibious	amphibious
alucidate	elucidate	amfitheatre	amphitheater
alum		amiable	
aluminum		amicable	
alumna		amiliorate	ameliorate
alure	allure	amity	
aluvial	alluvial	ammenable	amenable
amalgamate		ammonia	
amateur		ammunition	
amathyst	amethyst	amnesia	
amatory		amnesty	
amaze		amoeba/ameba	
ambassador		amorous	
ambedex-	ambidex-	amorphous	
terous	trous	amortize	
ambidextrous		ampersand	
ambiguity		amphetamine	
ambiguous		amphibian	
ambitious		amphibious	
ambivalence		amphitheater	
ambrosia		amplify	
ambulance		amputate	

amulet		anise	
amusement		aniversary	anniversary
anachronism		ankor	anchor
anaconda		annachronism	anachronism
analgesic		annaconda	anaconda
analogy		annalgesic	analgesic
analysis		annals	
analyze		anneal	
anarchy		annex	
anathema		annihilate	
anatomy		annimate	animate
ancellary	ancillary	anniversary	
ancestor		annoint	anoint
anchor		annonymous	anonymous
anchovy		annotate	
ancient		announcement	
ancillary		annoy	
androgen		annual	
androsterone		annuity	
anecdote		annul	
anelgesic	analgesic	annunciation (an-	
anemone		nouncement,	
anesthesia		see enunciation)	
anethma	anathema	anode	
aneurism		anoint	
anex	annex	anomaly	
angel (spirit)		anonymous	
angle (geome-		anotate	annotate
try/to fish)		anoy	annoy
angenue	ingenue/	answer	
	ingénue	ansy	antsy
anguish		ant (insect, see	
anicdote	anecdote	aunt)	
anilate	annihilate	antagonize	
animate		anteak	antique
animosity		antebiotic	antibiotic

antecedence		antiquarian	
antedate		antiquate	
antedote	antidote	antique	
antediluvian		antiquity	
antehistamine	antihistamine	antiroom	anteroom
antelope		anti-semitic	
antenna		antiseptic	
antepasto	antipasto	antisocial	
antequarian	antiquarian	antithesis	
antequate	antiquate	antitoxin	
anteque	antique	antsy	
anteroom		anunciation	annunciation
ante-semetic	anti-semitic	anurism	aneurism
anteseptic	antiseptic	anvil	
antetoxin	antitoxin	anxiety	
anthem		anxious	
anthology		aorta	
anthracite		apaplexy	apoplexy
anthropoid		aparatus	apparatus
anthropology		aparel	apparel
anthropomor-		aparent	apparent
phize		aparition	apparition
antibiotic		apartate	apartheid
antibody		apartheid	
antic		apartite	apartheid
anticedence	antecedence	apartment	
anticipate		apathy	
anticlimax		apeal	appeal
antidate	antedate	apear	appear
antideluvian	antediluvian	apeary	apiary
antidote		apease	appease
antihistamine		apeish	apish
antikuity	antiquity	apellate	appellate
antimacassar		apend	append
antipasto		apendage	appendage
antipathy		apendectomy	appendectomy

apendicitis	appendicitis	apothecary	
apendix	appendix	apothegm	
aperitef	aperitif	apotheosis	
aperitif		appall	
apertain	appertain	apparatus	
aperture		apparel	
apetite	appetite	apparent	
apeture	aperture	apparition	
apex		appartment	apartment
aphorism		appeal	
aphrodisiac		appear	
apierey	apiary	appease	
apiary		appellate	
apitomy	epitome	append	
apish		appendage	
aplaud	applaud	appendectomy	
aplause	applause	appendicitis	
apliance	appliance	appendix	
aplicable	applicable	appertain	
aplicator	applicator	appetite	
aplicatory	applicatory	applaud	
aplied	applied	applause	
aplique	applique	appliance	
aplomb		applicable	
aply	aptly	applicator	
apocalypse		applicatory	
apocryphal		applied	
apointment	appointment	applique	
apoll	appall	apponent	opponent
apology		appointment	
apolstry	upholstery	apportion	
apoplexy		appraise	
aportion	apportion	apprapo	apropos
apostle		appreciate	
apostrophe		apprehend	

apprentice		aquity	acuity
apprise		arabesque	
approach		arable	
approbation		araign	arraign
appropriate		arange	arrange
approval		arangutan	orangutan
approximate		arant	errant (travel-
appurtenance			ing, see
apraise	appraise		arrant)
apreciate	appreciate	aray	array
aprehend	apprehend	arbiter	
aprentice	apprentice	arbitrary	
a preori·	a priori	arbitrate	
apricot		arbor	
a priori		arbutus	
aprise	apprise	arc (curve, see	
aproach	approach	ark)	
aprobation	approbation	arcade	
apropos		arcaic	archaic
apropriate	appropriate	arcapelago	archipelago
aproval	approval	arcenal	arsenal
aproximate	approximate	arch	
apruval	approval	archaic	
aptitude		archeology	
aptly		archery	
apurtenance	appurtenance	archetype	
aqua		archipelago	
aquaint	acquaint	architect	
aquaintance	acquaintance	archives	
aquarium		arctic	
aquatic		ardachoke	artichoke
aqueduct		ardent	
aqueous		ardor	
aquiline		arduous	
aquittal	acquittal	arears	arrears

aregano	oregano	arrogate	
aresol	aerosol	arsenal	
argosy		arsenic	
argue		arson	
aria		artacal	article
arial	aerial	artachoke	artichoke
Arian	Aryan	artafac	artifact
arid		artafice	artifice
aristocracy		artaficial	artificial
arithmetic		artasan	artisan
ark (boat, see		arterial	
arc)		arteriosclerosis	
armada		artery	
armadillo		artesian well	
armament		arthritis	
armature		artic	arctic
armistice		artichoke	
armor		article	
arodynamics	aerodynamics	articulate	
arogance	arrogance	artifact	
arogate	arrogate	artifice	
aroma		artificial	
aronautics	aeronautics	artillery	
arora borealis	aurora	artisan	
	borealis	Aryan	
arouse		asail	assail
arpeggio		asassin	assassin
arraign		asatate	acetate
arrange		asault	assault
arrant (bad, see		asay	assay
errant)		asbestos	
array		ascance	askance
arrears		ascend	
arrest		ascension	
arrival		ascent (up, see	
arrogance		assent)	

ascertain		asma	asthma
ascetic (recluse,		asociation	association
see acetic)		asonance	assonance
ascettlin	acetylene	asort	assort
asciduous	assiduous	asparagus	
ascilloscope	oscilloscope	aspursion	aspersion
ascot tie		aspect	
ascribe		aspen	
ascription		asperity	
ascue	askew	aspersion	
asemble	assemble	asphalt	
asembly	assembly	asphyxiate	
asemetry	asymmetry	aspic	
asend	ascend	aspirant	
asent	assent	aspirate	
aseptic		aspire	
asert	assert	aspirin	
asertain	ascertain	assail	
asess	assess	assassin	
aset	asset	assault	
asetic	acetic	assay (analyze,	
asetlin	acetylene	see essay)	
asetone	acetone	assemble	
asetylene	acetylene	assembly	
asfalt	asphalt	assent (agree,	
asfixiate	asphyxiate	see ascent)	
asidious	assiduous	assert	
asign	assign	assess	
asignation	assignation	asset	
asiloscope	oscilloscope	assiduous	
asilum	asylum	assign	
asimilate	assimilate	assignation	
asinine		assimilate	
asistance	assistance	assinine	asinine
askance		assistance	
askew		(help)	

assistants		atest	attest
(helper)		atheist	
association		athlete	
assonance		atic	attic
assort		atire	attire
assuage	-	atitude	attitude
assume		atmosphere	
assure		atoll	
aster		atonal	
asterisk		atonement	
asteroid		atorney	attorney
asthma		atrabute	attribute
astigmatism		atractive	attractive
astral		atribute	attribute
astringent		atrition	attrition
astrology		atrocious	
astronaut		atrophy	
astronomy		attach	
astute		attache/attaché	
asuage	assuage	attack	
asume	assume	attain	
asunder		attainder	
asure	assure	attar	
asylum		attatude	attitude
asymmetry		attempt	
atach	attach	attendance	
atache	attache	attentive	
atain	attain	attenuate	
atainder	attainder	attest	
atar	attar	attic	
atavism		attire	
atempt	attempt	attitude	
atendance	attendance	attorney	
atentive	attentive	attractive	
atenuate	attenuate	attribute	

attrition
attune
atune   attune
atypical
auburn
auctioneer
audacious
audacity
audible
audience
audio-visual
audit
auditorium
auditory
auger (tool, see
  augur)
aught (small
  part, see
  ought)
augment
au gratin
augur (prophet,
  see auger)
augury
au lait
auld lang syne
au naturel
aunt (relation,
  see ant)
aura
aural (hearing,
  see oral)
aureole (halo,
  see oriole)
aureomycin

au revoir
auricle (outer
  ear, see
  oracle)
aurora borealis
auspices
auspicious
austere
authentic
authoritarian
authorize
autistic
autocracy
automation
automaton
autonomy
autopsy
autumn
auxiliary
avacado   avocado
available
avalanche
avant-garde
avarice
averdupois   avoirdupois
averse
aversion
avert
aviary
aviation
avid
avirdupois   avoirdupois
avocado
avocation
avoirdupois

awareness
away (distant,
  see aweigh)
awe
aweigh (nauti-
  cal, see away)
awful
awkward
awl (tool, see
  all)
awning
awry
axel (skating,
  see axial, axil,
  axle)

axial (forming
  axis, see axel,
  axil, axle)
axil (botany,
  see axel, axial,
  axle)
axiom
axis
axle (shaft, see
  axel, axial,
  axil)
axphyxiate   asphyxiate
aye (yes, see
  eye)
azalea
azure

B

babble

babushka

baccalaureate

bachelor

bacillus

bacteria

bacteriology

badger

badinage

badminton

baffle

bafoon   buffoon

bagatelle

bage   beige

bager   badger

bagetelle   bagatelle

begette   baguette

baggage

baggy

baguette

baige   beige

bail (scoop, see bale)

bailiff

bailiwick

bainful   baneful

bait (entice, see bate)

bakery

balance

balcony

bale (bundle, see bail)

balero   bolero

balestrade   balustrade

balewick   bailiwick

balk

balistic   ballistic

ballad

ballast

ballerina

ballet

ballistic

balloon

ballot

ballyhoo

balm

baloney/boloney		bare (naked,	
(slang, see		see bear)	
bologna)		bargain	
balsa		barge	
balsam		barister	barrister
balustrade		baritone	
bamboo		barley	
bamboozle		barnacle	
banal		barometer	
banana		baron (royalty,	
banaster	banister	see barren)	
bandage		baroque	
bandanna		barracks	
bandeau		barracuda	
banditry		barrage	
bandy		barrecuda	barracuda
baneful		barrel	
banish		barren (sterile,	
banister		see baron)	
bankrupt		barricade	
bankruptcy		barrier	
bannana	banana	barrister	
banquet		barrometer	barometer
banshee		barroom	
bantam		barter	
banter		basal (base, see	
baptize		basil)	
baracade	barricade	basal metabo-	
baracuda	barracuda	lism	
baratone	baritone	base (founda-	
barbarian		tion, see bass)	
barbecue		baserk	berserk
barber		bases (pl. of	
barbiturate		base, see	
barcarole		basis)	

bashful
basically
basil (plant, see
  basal)
basilica
basin
basinet (helmet,
  see bassinet)
basis (support,
  see bases)
basket
basmirch   besmirch
bas-relief
bass (music,
  see base)
basset hound
bassinet
  (cradle, see
  basinet)
bassoon
baste
bastille
bastion
batallion   battalion
batch
bate (lessen,
  see bait)
bathe
batiste
baton
battalion
batten
battery
bauble
bauer   bower

bauxite
bawd
bawling
bayonet
bayou
bazaar (market,
  see bizarre)
bazerk   berserk
bazooka
beach (shore,
  see beech)
beacon
beady
beagle
bear (animal,
  see bare)
beast
beastial   bestial
beat (hit, see
  beet)
beau (boy-
  friend, see
  bow)
beautify
beaux-arts
beaver
beckon
becoming
bedaub
bedlam
bedob   bedaub
Bedouin
bedraggled
beech (tree, see
  beach)

beecon	beacon	benaficial	beneficial
Beelzebub		benafit	benefit
beer (drink, see		beneath	
bier)		benediction	
beet (plant, see		benefactor	
beat)		beneficence	
befuddle		beneficial	
beggar		benefit	
begile	beguile	benevolence	
beginning		benidiction	benediction
begonia		benificial	beneficial
begrudge		benifit	benefit
beguile		benign	
behavior		benumb	
behest		Benzedrine	
beholden		benzine	
behoove		bequeath	
beige		bequest	
bekini	bikini	bereave	
belabor		beret	
belatedly		beriberi	
beleaguer		berometer	barometer
belero	bolero	berrage	barrage
belfry		berret	beret
believe		berry (fruit,	
belladonna		see bury)	
beligerent	belligerent	berserk	
bellacose	bellicose	berth (bed, see	
belles-lettres		birth)	
bellicose		berybery	beriberi
belligerent		beseeching	
bellows		besege	besiege
bellwether		beserk	berserk
Belzebub	Beelzebub	besiege	
bemuse		besmirch	

bestial	
bestow	
betray	
betroth	
betwixt	
bevel	
beverage	
bevy	
bewail	
beware	
bezerk	berserk
biannial	biennial
biannual	
bias	
bibliography	
bibliophile	
bibulous	
bicameral	
bicarbonate	
bicentennial	
biceps	
bide	
biege	beige
biennial	
bier (coffin, see beer)	
bifocal	
bigamy	
bight (bend, see bite)	
bigot	
bikini	
bilateral	
bilet	billet
bilinear	

bilingual	
bilious	
billed (invoice, see build)	
billet	
billet-doux	
billiards	
billious	bilious
billit	billet
billow	
bilous	bilious
binary	
binaural	
bindery	
binery	binary
binocular	
binoral	binaural
biosynthesis	
bipartisan	
bipartite	
birch	
birth (born, see berth)	
biscuit	
biseps	biceps
bison	
bisque	
bite (cut, see bight)	
bituminous	
bivouac	
bivwack	bivouac
bizarre (unusual, see bazaar)	

bladder		blurt	
blarney		boa constrictor	
blase/blasé		boar (pig, see	
blaser	blazer	bore)	
blason	blazon	boarder (guest,	
blasphemy		see border)	
blatant		boast	
blazer		bobalink	bobolink
blazon		bobble	bauble
bleak		bobbin	
bleary		bobolink	
bleat		bochalism	botulism
bleek	bleak	bode	
bleet	bleat	bodice	
blemish		bodlerize	bowdlerize
blert	blurt	bogey (spirit,	
blight		golf)	
blite	blight	boggle	
blithe		bogus	
blitzkrieg		boisenberry	boysenberry
blizzard		boisterous	
bloc (group,		bole (seed, see	
see block)		boll, bowl)	
bloch	blotch	bolero	
block (obstacle,		bolevard	boulevard
see bloc)		boll	
blockade		(tree, see bole,	
blossom		bowl)	
blotch		boll weevil	
blowsy		bologna (meat)	
blubber		boloney/baloney	
bludgeon		(slang)	
blueing/bluing		bolster	
blugeon	bludgeon	bombard	
blunderbuss		bombast	
blurb		bona fide	

bonanza
bondage
bonet   bonnet
boney   bony
bonfire
bonnet
bonny (good,
   see bony)
bonus
bon voyage
bony (of bone,
   see bonny)
booby trap
bookkeeping
boomerang
boondoggle
boorish
booster
bootee (infant's
   sock, see booty)
bootonniere   boutonniere
booty (spoils,
   see bootee)
booze
boquet   bouquet
borax
bordello
border (boun-
   dary, see
   boarder)
bore (puncture,
   see boar)
boric acid
born (birth)
borne (carried)
boron

borough (town,
   see burro,
   burrow)
borrow
borscht
bosom
bossy
botany
botch
botchulism   botulism
botulism
boucle
boudoir
bo weevil   boll weevil
bough (main
   branch, see
   bow)
bouillabaise
bouillon (soup,
   see bullion)
boulder
boulevard
boundary
boundless
bounteous
bouquet
bourbon
bourgeois
boutonniere
bovine
bow (submit,
   see bough)
bow (curve, see
   beau)
bowel
bower

bowery		brazen	
bowl (dish, see		brazier	brassiere/
bole, boll)			brassière
boxite	bauxite	breach (break,	
boy (male		see breech)	
child, see		bread (food,	
buoy)		see bred)	
boycott		breadth (width,	
boysenberry		see breath)	
bracelet		break (destroy,	
bracket		see brake)	
brackish		breakfast	
braggadocio		breath (respiration,	
braid		see breadth)	
Braille		breathe	
braise (cook-		breathern	brethren
ing, see		bred (p.t.,	
braze)		breed; see	
brake (stop,		bread)	
see break)		breech (gun,	
bramble		see breach)	
brandish		breeches	
brandy		breed	
brasen	brazen	breeze	
brassiere/		breif	brief
brassière		brethren	
bravado		brevet	
bravery		breviary	
bravo		brevit	brevet
bravura		brevity	
brawl		brewery	
brawny		briar (pipe, see	
braze (solder-		brier)	
ing, see		bric-a-brac	
braise)		bricket	briquette

bridal (of a wedding, see bridle)		brontosaurus	
bridge		brooch (jewelry, see broach)	
bridle (harness, see bridal)		broshure	brochure
brief		brothel	
brier (plant, see briar)		browbeat	
		browse	
brig		bruise	
brigade		brunette	
brigadier		brusque	
brigand		brutal	
brilliance	brillance	bubonic plague	
brine		buccaneer	
brior	briar (pipe)	buccaroo	buckaroo
	brier (plant)	buckaroo	
briquette		bucket	
brisket		bucolic	
brissle	bristle	budge	
bristle		budget	
brittle		buffalo	
broach (mention, see brooch)		buffer	
		buffet	
		buffoon	
broad		bugaboo	
brocade		bugle	
broccoli		build (construct, see billed)	
brochure		bulevard	boulevard
brocoli	broccoli	bullet	
brogue		bulletin	
brokerage		bullion (gold, see bouillon)	
bromide			
bronchial		bulwark	
broncobuster		bumpkin	

bumptious
bungalow
bungle
bunion
bunyon   bunion
buoy (float,
  see boy)
bur/burr
burbon   bourbon
burch   birch
burden
bureau
bureaucracy
burette
burgeois   bourgeois
burgeoning
burglar
burial
burlesque
burley
  (tobacco)
burly
  (strong)
burnish
burnt
burr/bur

burro (don-
  key, see
  borough,
  burrow)
burrow (dig,
  see borough,
  burro)
bursar
bury (cover,
  see berry)
bushel
business
bustle
but (con-
  junction,
  see butt)
butcher
butt (ram,
  see but)
butte
buttock/buttocks
button
buttress
burzhwa   bourgeois
buzzard
byfocal   bifocal
byou   bayou

C

cabal

cabaret

cabbage

cabinet

cable

caboose

cache (hiding
   place, see
   cash)

cachet

cackle

cacoon   cocoon

cacophony

cactus

cadaver

caddish

cadence

cafeteria

caffeine

cagey

caisson

cajole

calaboose

calamine

calamity

calcedony   chalcedony

calandar   calendar

calcify

calcimine

calcium

calculate

calculous
   (pathology)

calculus (math)

caldron/cauldron

cale   kale

calendar

calerie   calorie

calesthenics   calisthenics

caliber

calico

caliph

calisthenics

calligraphy

callous
   (thickened,
   see callus)

callow

callus (skin, see
   callous)

calorie		cannibal	
calsify	calcify	cannon (gun,	
calumny		see canon)	
calypso		cannot	
camaflage	camouflage	canny	
camaraderie		canoe	
cameleon	chameleon	canon (church	
camellia		law, see	
cameo		cannon)	
camfer	camphor	canopy (cover,	
camisole		see canapé)	
cammemorate	commemo-	cansel	cancel
	rate	cantaloupe	
camode	commode	cantankerous	
camomile		cantata	
camouflage		canteen	
campaign		canter (talker,	
camphor		see cantor)	
canal		canticle	
canapé (toast,		cantilever	
see canopy)		canto	
canard		canton	
canary		cantor (choir-	
canasta		leader, see	
cancel		canter)	
candescence		canvas	
candidate		(material)	
candle		canvass	
candor		(inquire)	
carnige	carnage	canyon	
canine		caos	chaos
canister		capacious	
canker		caper	
cannery		capillary	

capital (money,		cardiogram	
seat of govern-		carisma	charisma
ment)		cardsharp	
capitol (building)		careen	
capitulate		career	
capon		caress	
caprice		caret (printing,	
capricious		see carat,	
capsule		carrot, karat)	
captain		caribou	
caption		caricature	
captivate		caries (decay,	
captor		see carries)	
caracature	caricature	carillon	
caramel		carmel	caramel
carasel	carrousel	carmine	
carat (weight,		carnage	
see caret,		carnal	
carrot, karat)		carnival	
caravan		carnivore	
carberator	carburetor	carode	corrode
carbide		carol (song, see	
carbine		carrel)	
carbohydrate		carosion	corrosion
carbon		carousal	
carbuncle		(drunken	
carburetor		revel, see car-	
carabou	caribou	rousel)	
carcass		carping	
carcinoma		carrel (a study,	
cardiac		see carol)	
cardigan		carriage	
cardinal		carries (trans-	
carecature	caricature	ports, see caries)	

carrion		castanet	
carrot		caste (rank, see	
(vegetable,		cast)	
see carat,		caster (stand,	
caret, karat)		see castor)	
carrousel		castigate	
(merry-go-		castle	
round, see		castor (beaver,	
carousal)		see caster)	
cartage		casualty	
carte blanche		catachism	catechism
cartilage		cataclysm	
cartography		catacomb	
carton		catacumen	catechumen
cartoon		catagory	category
cartridge		catalepsy	
casarean	cesarean	catalog/	
caserole	casserole	catalogue	
cascade		catalpa	
casein		catalyst	
cash (money,		catarpillar	caterpillar
see cache)		catapult	
cashew nut		cataract	
cashier		catarrh	
cashmere		catastrophe	
casia	cassia	catatonic	
casino		catechism	
casket		catechumen	
casm	chasm	catecomb	catacomb
cason	caisson	category	
casserole		catelepsy	catalepsy
cassia		catelog	catalog/
	casino		catalogue
cassock		catelyst	catalyst
cast (throw,		cater	
see caste)		cateract	cataract

cater-corner/
  kitty-corner
caterpillar
catharsis
cathedral
catheter
cathexis
cathode
Catholic
catsup/ketchup
cattalyst   catalyst
catty
catydid   katydid
caucus
caudal (tail)
caudle (drink)
cauldron/caldron
cauliflower
causal
caustic
cauterize
cautious
cavalcade
cavalier
cavalryman
caviar
cavil
cavity
cavort
cease
cedar
cede (grant,
  see seed)
cefalic   cephalic
ceiling
celebrate

celebrity
celerity
celery
celestial
celibate
celuloid   celluloid
cellar (under-
  ground room,
  see seller)
cello
cellophane
cellular
celluloid
cellulose
celophane   cellophane
cement
cemetery
cense (to per-
  fume, see
  cents, scents,
  sense)
censer (vessel,
  see censor)
censor (official,
  see censer)
censure
census (popu-
  lation, see
  senses)
cent (penny,
  see scent,
  sent)
centaur
centenary
centennial
centigrade

centimeter
centrifugal
centipetal
cents (pl.
  pennys, see
  cense, scents,
  sense)
centurion
century (100
  years, see
  sentry)
cephalic
cepia   sepia
ceramics
cereal (food,
  see serial)
cerebellum
cerebral
cerebral palsy
cerebrum
ceremony
cerise
cermudgeon   curmudgeon
cerosis   cirrhosis
cerrated   serrated
certatude   certitude
certificate
certify
certiorari
certitude
cerulean
cervix
cessation
cession (yield-
  ing, see
  session)

cesspool
chafe
chaff
chagrin
chairman
chaise longue
chalcedony
chalee   challis
chalet
chalice
challenge
challis
chamberlain
chambray
chameleon
chamfer
chamise   chemise
chamois
champagne
  (wine)
champaign
  (plan)
chancel
chancellor
chancery
chandelier
channel
chantey (song,
  see shanty)
chanticleer
Chantilly
Chanukah/
  Hanukkah
chaos
chaparral
chapeau

chapel		cheif	chief
chaperon		chello	cello
chaplain		chemise	
chapter		chenille	
character		cherish	
charade		cheroot	
charcoal		cherub	
charicature	caricature	chervil	
chariot		chevalier	
charisma		chevron	
charivari		chic (stylish,	
charlatan		see sheik)	
charnel		chicanery	
chartreuse		chicano	
charwoman		chickadee	
chary		chicory	
chasee	chassis	chief	
chased (pur-		chiffon	
sued, see		chiffonier	
chaste)		chigger	
chase longe	chaise longue	chignón	
chasm		Chihuahua	
chassis		chime	
chaste (pure,		chimera	
see chased)		chimney	
chastise		chimpanzee	
chastity		chinchilla	
chateau/		chintz	
château		chiropody	
chatelaine		chiropractor	
chattel		chisel	
chatty		chivalry	
chauffeur		chiwawa	Chihuahua
chauvinism		chlorine	
cheetah		chloroform	
chef		chlorophyll	

chocolate		cicada	
choffeur	chauffeur	cieling	ceiling
choir (singers,		cigar	
see quire)		cigarette	
choke		cinamon	cinnamon
cholera		cinch	
choleric		cinder	
cholesterol		cinema	
choral (singers,		cinic	cynic
see coral,		cinnabar	
corral)		cinnamon	
chord (music,		cintillate	scintillate
see cord)		cipher (code,	
choreography		see sypher)	
chortle		circuit	
chovinism	chauvinism	circular	
chrisanthemum	chrysanthe-	circumcise	
	mum	circumference	
christen		circumflex	
chromatic		circumlocution	
chrome		circumscribe	
chromium		circumspect	
chronic		circumstance	
chronicle		circumvent	
chronological		circut	circuit
chronology		ciropractor	chiropractor
chrysalis		cirrhosis	
chrysanthemum		cirriculum	curriculum
churlish		cirrocumulus	
chute (slide,		cirrostratus	
see shoot)		cirrus	
churvil	chervil	cisegy	syzygy
Chyanne	Cheyenne	cist (chest,	
cianamide	cyanamide	see cyst)	
cianide	cyanide	cistern	

citadel		cleft palate	
citation		clemency	
cite (quote, see		clense	cleanse
sight, site)		cleptomaniac	kleptomaniac
citology	cytology	clerical	
civet		cliche/cliché	
civic		click (sound,	
civility		see clique)	
clack (noise,		clientele	
see claque)		cliff	
clairvoyance		climb (ascent)	
clammy		clime (climate)	
clamor		clinic	
clandestine		clique (clan,	
clangor		see click)	
claque		clobber	
(applauders,		cloche	
see clack)		cloisonne	
claret		cloister	
clarevoyance	clairvoyance	cloraform	chloroform
clarify		cloraphyll	chlorophyll
clarinet		clorine	chlorine
clarion		closet	
clarity		closh	cloche
classify		colesterol	cholesterol
clatter		clostraphobia	claustrophobia
claustrophobia		closure	
clavichord		cloth	
clavicle		clothe	
cleanse		clothes	
cleat		clothier	
cleave		clout	
cleche	cliche/	cluster	
	cliché	clutch	
clef		coafficient	coefficient

coagulate
coalesce
coalition
coarse (rough,
  see corse,
  course)
coax
cobbler
cobra
cocaine
coccyx
cockatoo
cockleshell
cockney
cocksiks   coccyx
cocoa
cocoon
coddle
co-defendant
codeine
codger
codicil
codify
coefficient
coerce
coessential
coffers
coffin
cofrere   confrere
cogent
coger   codger
cogitate
cognac
cognate
cognition

cognizant
cohere
cohesion
cohort
coiffure
coign (corner,
  see coin,
  quoin)
coin (money,
  see coign,
  quoin)
coincide
coincidence
coition
coitus
colander
colate   collate
colateral   collateral
colembine   columbine
colera   cholera
colesterol   cholesterol
colic
colide   collide
coliflower   cauliflower
coliseum/
  Colosseum
colision   collision
collaborate
collapse
collate
collateral
colleague
collide
collie
colliery

colliflower	cauliflower	commandant	
collision		commandeer	
colloid		commando	
colloquial		commemorate	
colloquy		commence	
collude		commend	
colofon	colophon	commensurate	
cologne		commentary	
coloid	colloid	commentator	
colon		commerce	
colonel (officer,		commercial	
see kernel)		commingle	
colonnade		commiserate	
colony		commissar	
colophon		commissary	
coloquial	colloquial	commission	
coloquy	colloquy	commit	
colossal		committee	
Colosseum/		commode	
coliseum		commodious	
colossus		commodity	
colude	collude	commodore	
columbine		commondeer	commandeer
column		commotion	
collumnar		communal	
coma		commune	
combat		communicate	
comedian		communion	
comedienne		communique/	
comedy		communiqué	
comet		communist	
comeuppance		community	
comfortable		comuppance	comeuppance
comma		commute	
command		comparative	

compassionate	comprise	
compatible	compromise	
compel	comptometer	
compelled	comptroller/	
compensate	controller	
compete	compulsion	
competence	compunction	
competition	computer	
competitor	comrade	
complacent	conaseur	connoisseur
(self-satisfied,	conceal	
see complai-	concede	
sant)	conceit	
complain	conceive	
complaisant	concent	consent
(amiable, see	concentrate	
complacent)	concentric	
complement	concept	
(to add, see	concer	concur
compliment)	concern	
complete	concert	
complexion	concertina	
compliant	concerto	
complicate	concession	
complicity	concherto	concerto
compliment	concieve	conceive
(praise, see	conciliate	
complement)	concise	
component	conclude	
compose	concoct	
composite	concomitant	
composition	concord	
compositor	concourse	
comprehend	concrete	
compress	concubine	

concupiscent
concur
concussion
condement   condiment
condemn
condense
condenser
condescend
condiment
condole
condone
condor
conduce
conduct
conduit
conefer   conifer
coneseur   connoisseur
confer
confess
confetti
confidant (trusted
  person)
confident (self
  assured)
confiscate
conflagration
confrere
confuse
conga
congeal
congenial
congenital
congest
conglomerate

congratulate
congregate
congruent
conic
conifer
conjagate   conjugate
conjecture
conjest   congest
conjugal
conjugate
conjure
connect
connesseur   connoisseur
conniption
connive
connoisseur
connote
connubial
conquer
conquistador
consanance   consonance
consanguinity
conscience
conscientious
conscious
conscript
consecrate
consecutive
consensus
consent
consequence
conservative
conservatory
conserve

consign		contempt
consistent		contend
console		conterminous
consolidate		context
consomme/		contiguous
consommé		continence
consonance		(self-restraint,
conspicuous		see counte-
conspiracy		nance)
conspirator		continent
conspire		contingent
constabulary		continual
constapated	constipated	continuity
constellation		continuum
consternation		contort
constipated		contour
constituency		contraband
constitute		contraception
constrain		contract
constrict		contradict
construe		contralto
consul		contrary
consume		contravene
consummate		contrite
consumme	consomme/	contrive
	consommé	controller/
consumption		comptroller
contact		controversy
contagion		controvert
container		contumacious
contaminate		contusion
contata	cantata	conundrum
contemacious	contuma-	convalescence
	cious	convene
contemplate		convenience
contemporary		converge

converse		cordon	
conversion		cordovan	
converter		corduroy	
convict		core (center,	
convince		see corps,	
convivial		corpse)	
convocation		corelate	correlate
convolesence	convalescence	corener	coroner
convolution		corenet	coronet
convulse		coreography	chore-
conyac	cognac		ography
coo (bill and...,		corespond	correspond
see coup)		corespondent	
cookery		(adulterer,	
coolie		see corre-	
coop (for		spondent)	
chickens)		corgel	cordial
co-op (for		coriander	
people)		cormorant	
cooperage		cornea	
cooperate		cornet (horn, see	
co-opt		coronet)	
coordinate		cornice	
copious		cornucopia	
copulate		coroborate	corroborate
coquette		corode	corrode
corador	corridor	corollary	
coral (sea ani-		corona	
mal, see		coronary	
choral, corral)		coronation	
coranary	coronary	coroner	
coranation	coronation	coronet (crown,	
cord (string,		see cornet)	
see chord)		corosion	corrosion
cordial		corporal (soldier,	
cordisone	cortisone	see corporeal)	

201016

corporate	cosmos
corporeal (physi- cal, see corporal)	costic	caustic
corps (unit, see core, corpse)	costume
	cotage	cottage
corpse (body, see core, corps)	coterie
	cotillion
	cottage
	cougar
corpulent	council (meeting)
corpuscle	counsel (advise)
corral (pen, see choral, coral)	countenance (expression, see continence)
corraner	coroner
correlate	coup (master- stroke, see coo)
correspond
correspondence (letter)	coup d'etat/ coup d'état
correspondents (reporters)	coupé
	coupon
corridor	courageous
corroborate	courier
corrode	course (direc- tion, see coarse)
corrosion
corrupt
corsage	courteous
corsair	courtesan
corset	courtesy
cortege	couturier
corterize	cauterize	covenant
cortisone	covert
corupt	corrupt	covey
cosmetic	coward
cosmology	cowtow	kowtow
cosmopolitan	coxix	coccyx

COYOTE   CROISSANTS

coyote		creosote	
crabby		crepe	
cradential	credential	crescendo	
cradle		crescent	
crag		cresh	creche/
crampon			chèche
cranberry		creshendo	crescendo
cranial		cretin	
cranny		crevasse	
crape	crepe	crevice	
crashe	creche/crechè	cribbage	
cratique	critique	cricket	
cravat		crier	
crayon		criminal	
creak (sound, see creek)		crimson	
creamery		cringe	
creap	creep	crinkle	
crease		crinoline	
creasol	creosol	cripple	
creasote	creosote	cript	crypt
creature		criptic	cryptic
creche/crèche		cripton	krypton
credence		crisis	
credential		crispy	
credible		cristal	crystal
credo		criterion	
credulity		criticism	
credulous		critique	
creek (stream, see creak)		croak	
creep		crochet	
cremate		crotchety	
creole		crockery	
creosol		crocodile	
		crocus	
		croissants	

croft		crusible	crucible
croke	croak	crusifix	crucifix
crokus	crocus	crusify	crucify
cromatic	chromatic	crustacean	
crome	chrome	crutch	
cromium	chromium	crux	
crony		cryer	crier
croquet		crypt	
croquette		cryptic	
crone (old		crypton	krypton
woman, see		crysanthenium	chrysanthe-
krone)			mum
cronic	chronic	crystal	
cronological	chronological	cubical (cube	
crooton	crouton	shaped)	
croshay	crochet	cubicle (en-	
crouch		closure)	
croup		cuboard	cupboard
croupier		cuckold	
crouton		cuckoo	
crovat	cravat	cuddle	
crucial		cudgel	
crucible		cudle	cuddle
crucifix		cue (poolstick,	
crucify		see queue)	
cruel		cugar	cougar
cruet		cugel	cudgel
cruise (voyage,		cuisine	
see cruse)		cul-de-sac	
cruller		culee	coolie
crumble		culinary	
crusade		culminate	
cruse (jar, see		culottes	
cruise)		culpable	
crusial	crucial	cultivate	

cumbersome		curt	
cumin		curtailment	
cum laude		curtain	
cummerbund		curteous	courteous
cumulative		curtesy	courtesy
cumulus		curtsy	
cumquat	kumquat	cushion	
cuneiform		cuspidor	
cunning		cussedness	
cupboard		custard	
cupidity		custody	
cupola		customary	
cupon	coupon	cutaneous	
curacao/		cuticle	
curaçao		cutlass	
curate		cutlery	
curator		cuturier	couturier
curdle		cyanamide	
curette		cyanide	
curfew		cycle	
curiculum	curriculum	cycletron	cyclotron
curier	courier	cycloid	
curious		cyclometer	
curlicue		cyclone	
curmudgeon		cyclopedia	
currant (berry,		cynch	cinch
see current)		cyclotron	
currate	curate	cygnet (swan,	
currator	curator	see signet)	
current		cylinder	
(present, see		cymbal (music,	
currant)		see symbol)	
curriculum		cynic	
curry		cyote	coyote
cursory		cypher	cipher

cypress		cystalic	systalic
cysegy	syzygy	cytology	
cyst (growth, see cist)		czar/tsar	

D

dabble		damn (con-	
dabut	debut	demn, see	
Dachshund		dam)	
dacollete	decollete/	damsel	
	décolleté	dandelion	
dacor	decor/décor	dandruff	
Dacron		dane	deign
daffodil		dangle	
dagerotype	daguerreo-	danoman	denouement
	type	dapper	
dagger		daring	
daguerreotype		dashboard	
dahlia		dastardly	
dainty		daub	
dairy (milk		dauntless	
farm, see		dauphin	
diary)		dawdle	
daisy		daze	
dakshund	Dachshund	dazzle	
dalia	dahlia	deacon	
dally		deaf	
dam (block,		deam	deem
see damn)		dearth	
damage		debacle	
damask		debasement	

debauch		declivity	
debenture		decollete/	
debetor	debtor	décolleté	
debilitate		decompose	
debit		decon	deacon
deboch	debauch	decontaminate	
debonair		decor/décor	
debris		decorate	
debtor		decorous	
debunk		decorum	
debut		decrepit	
decadence		dedicate	
decal		deduce	
decanter		deem	
decapitate		defecate	
decathlon		defenite	definite
deceased		defense	
decedence	decadence	defer	
deceit		deference	
deceive		deferential	
decelerate		deffuse	diffuse
decent		defiance	
deception		deficiency	
decerous	decorous	deficit	
decibel		definite	
decide		definitive	
deciduous		deflower	
decieve	deceive	defray	
decimal		deft	
decimate		defunct	
decipher		defy	
decision		degenerate	
decisive		dehumidify	
declamation		dehydrate	
declension		deify	

deign		demise	
deity		demitasse	
delapidated	dilapidated	demiurge	
delectable		demobilize	
delegate		democracy	
delemma	dilemma	demolish	
deleterious		demonetize	
deliberate		demonstrate	
delicate		demoralize	
delicious		demur (objec-	
delineate		tion)	
delinquency		demure (re-	
delinquent		served)	
delirious		dendrite	
delirium		denem	denim
delude		denigrate	
deluge		denim	
delute	dilute	denizen	
deluxe		denominator	
demagnetize		denouement/	
demagogue		dénouement	
deman	demesne	dense	
demask	damask	denunciate	
demean		deodorant	
demeanor		deoxidize	
demension	dimension	depaty	deputy
dementia		dependent	
precox		depict	
demerit		depilatory	
demeurge	demiurge	deplete	
demesne		depolarize	
demilitarize		depopulate	
deminish	diminish	deportation	
deminution	diminution	deposition	
deminutive	diminutive	depository	

depot
depravation
  (corruption,
  see depriva-
  tion)
deprecate
depreciate
depredation
depressant
depression
deprivation
  (loss, see
  depravation)
deputy
derelict
derick   derrick
dering-do   derring-do
derivation
dermatology
derogate
derogatory
derrick
derring-do
derrogate   derogate
derth   dearth
dervish
descant
descend
descendant
descern   discern
desciple   disciple
describe
desease   disease
desecrate
desegregate

desel   diesel
desend   descend
desendant   descendant
desensitize
desert (arid,
  see dessert)
desible   decible
desiccate
desicrate   desecrate
desideratum
design
designate
desirable
desist
desolate
Desopxyn
despair
desparage   disparage
desperado
desperate
despicable
despise
despite
despondence
despot
dessert (food,
  see desert)
destination
destine
destiny
destitute
destroy
destruction
desuetude
desultory

detach		dewy	
detail		Dexedrine	
detain		dexterity	
deter		dextrose	
deterent	deterrent	diabetes	
detergent		diabolic	
deteriorate		diacese	diocese
determine		diadem	
deterrent		diafanous	diaphanous
dethrone		diafragm	diaphragm
detonate		diagnose	
detor	debtor	diagnosis	
detour		diagonal	
detract		diagraming	
detriment		dial	
deuce		dialect	
devaluate		dialogue	
devastate		diameter	
develop		diametric	
deviate		diamond	
device (invention,		diaper	
see devise)		diaphanous	
devide	divide	diaphragm	
devine	divine	diarrhea	
devinity	divinity	diary (record,	
devisible	divisible	see dairy)	
devisor	divisor	diathermy	
devorce	divorce	diatribe	
devious		dice	
devise (plan,		dichotomy	
see device)		dickey	
devitalize		dictate	
devolve		dictionary	
devour		dictum	
devout		didactic	

die (death, see
  dye)
diedem   diadem
diesel
differ
difference
differential
differentiate
difficult
diffidence
diffract
diffuse
digestible
digit
digital
digitalis
dignify
dignitary
dignity
digress
dilapidated
dilatante   dilettante
dilate
dilatory
dilemma
dilettante
diligence
dilicious   delicious
dillydally
dilute
dimension
diminish
diminution
diminutive
dimity
dinasaur   dinosaur

diner (restaurant,
  see dinner)
dinette
dinghy
dinner (meal,
  see diner)
dinosaur
diocese
diorama
dioxide
diper   diaper
diphtheria
diphthong
diploma
diplomacy
dipper
dipsomania
diptheria   diphtheria
dipthong   diphthong
directorate
directory
dirge
dirigible
dirndl
dirth   dearth
disability
disabille   dishabille
disaffection
disaffirm
disallow
disappear
disappoint
disapprobation
disapprove
disarmament
disarming

disarrange		discrepancy	
disarray		discrete (distinct,	
disassemble		see discreet)	
disassociate		discretion	
disaster		discribe	describe
disastrous		discriminate	
disavow		discursive	
disbelieve		discurteous	discourteous
disburse		discus (disk)	
disc/disk		discuss (talk)	
discard		discussion	
disceminate	disseminate	disdain	
discern		disect	dissect
discernible		disease	
discheveled	disheveled	disembark	
discidence	dissidence	disembody	
disciple		disembowel	
disciplinary		disenchant	
discipline		disencumber	
disclaimer		disenfranchise	
discomfit		disengage	
discomfort		disension	dissension
discomposure		disentanglement	
disconcerting		disentery	dysentery
disconnect		disesteem	
disconsolate		disfunction	dysfunction
discontinue		disgorge	
discordant		disgruntled	
discourage		disguise	
discourse		disgusting	
discourteous		dishabille	
discoverable		disharmony	
discovery		dishearten	
discreditable		disheveled	
discreet (tactful,		dishonesty	
see discrete)		disillusion	

disinclined		disrupt	
disinfect		dissanance	dissonance
disingenuous		dissapate	dissipate
disinherit		dissatisfy	
disintegrate		dissect	
disinter		dissemble	
disk/disc		disseminate	
dismal		dissension	
dismantle		dissent	
dismiss		dissentient	
disobedience		dissern	discern
disobey		dissertation	
disobliging		disservice	
disoriented		dissheveled	disheveled
dispair	despair	dissidence	
disparage		dissimilar	
disparate		dissimilate	
dispassionate		(unlike)	
dispatch		dissimulate	
dispel		(conceal)	
dispensable		dissipate	
dispensary		dissociate	
dispenser		dissolute	
dispepsia	dyspepsia	dissolution	
disperse		dissolve	
dispicable	despicable	dissonance	
dispirited		dissuade	
dispise	despise	dissymmetry	
dispite	despite	distaff	
displease		distance	
dispose		distemper	
dispossess		distinct	
disproportion		distinguished	
disregard		distort	
disrepair		distortion	
disrepute		distract	

distrait		dollop	
distraught		dolly	
distribution		dolorous	
distrophie	dystrophy	dolphin	
disturbance		doltish	
ditty		domain	
diurnal		domicile	
divan		dominant	
diverge		domineer	
divers		dominion	
diverse		domino	
divide		donate	
dividend		donkey	
divine		donor	
divinity		donut	doughnut
divisible		doodle	
division		dormant	
divisor		dormitory	
divorce		dormouse	
divot		dorsal	
divulge		dory	
divurge		dosage	
divvy		dosea	dossier
Doberman		doshund	dachshund
pinscher		dossier	
docia	dossier	dote	
docile		douche	
docket		doughnut	
document		dour	
doddering		douse	
dodge		dowager	
doggerel		dowdy	
dogma		dowel	
doily		dower	
doldrums		dowry	
doleful		doxology	

doze
drachma
draft/draught
dragon
drapery
draught/draft
drawl
drawn
drayage
dreary
dredge
dribble
driblet
drivel
drizzle
droll
dromedary
drone
droopy
dropsy
drought/drouth
drowsy
drudge
druid
drunkard
drunkenness
dual (two, see
  duel)
dubious
ducal
ducat
duce   deuce
duche   douche
duchess

duchy
ductile
dudgeon
duel (contest,
  see dual)
duet
duffel bag
duffer
dukedom
dulcet
dulcimer
dumbbell
dumfound
dungaree
dungeon
duodenum
duplicate
duplicity
durable
duration
duress
durndl   dirndl
dwarf
dwindle
dye (coloring,
  see die)
dynamic
dynamite
dynamo
dynasty
dysentery
dysfunction
dyspepsia
dystrophy

E

eager		ecstatic	
eagle		ectoderm	
eak	eke	ectomorph	
easel		ectoplasm	
eavesdrop		ecumenical	
ebet	abet	eczema	
ebony		eddy	
ebullient		edefication	edification
eccentric		edefice	edifice
ecclesiastical		edefy	edify
eccumenical	ecumenical	edelweiss	
echelon		edgy	
echo		edible	
eclair		edict	
eclectic		edification	
eclesiastical	ecclesiastical	edifice	
eclipse		edify	
eclogue		Edipus	Oedipus
ecology		edition	
ecologist		editor	
economic		editorial	
economy		education	
ecru		educator	
ecsentric	eccentric	educe	
ecstasy		edy	eddy

eek	eke	eighteen	
eerie		eighth	
efedrine	ephedrine	eightieth	
efemeral	ephemeral	eighty	
efeminate	effeminate	eire	eyre
efervescence	effervescence	either	
efete	effete	ejaculate	
efface		eject	
effect (conclu-		eke	
sion, see affect)		elaborate	
effectual		elagiac	elegiac
effeminate		elagize	elegize
effervescence		elagy	elegy
effete		elament	element
efficacious		elamental	elemental
efficacy		elamentary	elementary
efficient		elamosynary	eleemosynary
effigy		elan/élan	
effort		elaphant	elephant
effrontery		elaphantine	elephantine
effusion		elapse	
effusive		elastic	
eficacy	efficacy	elate	
eficient	efficient	elation	
egalitarian		elavate	elevate
ego		elavation	elevation
egocentric		elavator	elevator
egoism		elbow	
egotism		elderberry	
egotistical		elderly	
egregious		electoral	
egress		electorate	
egret		electric	
eguana	iguana	electrocardiogram	
eider down		electrocute	

electrode
electrodynamics
electrolysis
electrolytic
electromagnetic
electron
electronic
electroplate
electrotherapy
eleemosynary
elegance
elegible   eligible
elegibility   eligibility
elegiac
elegize
elegy
element
elemental
elementary
elephant
elephantine
elequence   eloquence
elete   elite
elevate
elevation
elevator
eleven
elfin
elicit (evoke,
   see illicit)
elide
eligibility
eligible
eliminate
elipse   ellipse

elipsis   ellipsis
elision
elite
elixir
ellipse
ellipsis
elocution
elongate
elope
eloquence
elucidate
elude (avoid,
   see allude)
elusion (escape,
   see illusion)
elusive
emaciate
emaciation
emanate
emanation
emancipate
emasculate
embalm
embankment
embargo
embark
embarkation
embarrass
embassy
embattle
embed
embellish
ember
embezzlement
embilical cord   umbilical cord

embitter
emblazon
emblem
emblematic
embody
embolden
emboss
embrace
embroider
embroidery
embroil
embryo
embryology
embryonic
emcee/M.C.
emegra   emigre/émigré
emend (change,
  see amend)
emerald
emerge
emergency
emeritus
emersion (coming
  forth, see
  immersion)
emery
emetic
emigrant
emigrate (place
  to place, see
  immigrate)
emigration
emigre/émigré
eminent (promi-
  nent, see imma-
  nent, imminent)

emissary
emission
emit
emollient
emolument
emotion
empathy
Emperin   Empirin
empetigo   impetigo
emperor
emphasis
emphasize
emphatic
empire
empirean   empyrean
empiric
empirical
empiricism
Empirin
emplacement
employ
employable
employe/
  employee
emporium
empower
empresario   impresario
empyrean
emulate
emulsify
emulsion
enable
enactment
enamel
enamored
encampment

encephalitis		energize	
encephalogram		energy	
enchant		enervate (sap	
encircle		vitality, see	
enclasp		innervate)	
enclave		enfeeble	
enclose/inclose		enforce	
enclosure		enfranchise	
encomium		engage	
encompass		engender	
encore		English	
encounter		engine	
encourage		engineer	
encroach		engrave	
encrust		engross	
encumber		engulf	
encumbrance		enhance	
encyclical		enharmonic	
encyclopedia		enigma	
encyst		enigmatic	
endanger		enjoin	
endear		enlightenment	
endeavor		enlist	
endemic		enliven	
endive		en masse	
endocrine		enmesh/inmesh	
endocrinology		enmity	
endorse		ennoble	
endowment		ennui	
endue/indue		enormous	
endurance		enormity	
endure		enomaly	anomaly
enebriate	inebriate	enough	
enema		enplane	
enemy		enrage	
energetic		enrapture	

enrich		entry
enroll		entwine
en route		enumerate
ensconce		enunciate
ensemble		enunciation (pro-
enshrine		nunciation, see
enshroud		annunciation)
ensign		envelop (enclose)
enslave		envelope
ensue		(wrapper)
entail		envelopment
entangle		envenom
enterprise		enviable
entertain		envious
enth degree	nth degree	environment
enthrall		environmental
enthrone		environs
enthusiasm		envisage
enthusiast		envision
enthusiastic		envoy
entice		envy
entirely		enwrap
entirety		enzyme
entitle		eon
entity		epathet	epithet
entomology		epaulet
entourage		epetaph	epitaph
entrails		ephedrine
entrance		ephemeral
entrant		Epifany	Epiphany
entreat		epic
entree		epicure
entrenchment		epicurean
entrepreneur		epidemic
entrust		epidermis

epigram	equivocate	
epigrammatic	era	
epilepsy	eradicate	
epileptic	eradicator	
epilogue	erand	errand
Epiphany	erant	errant
Episcopalian	erase	
episode	eraser	
epistle	erasure	
epitaph	erate	aerate
epithet	eratic	erratic
epitome	eratum	erratum
epitomize	erb	herb
epoch	erect	
epochal	erecter	
epprobrious opprobrious	erection	
equable	ergo	
equal	erie	eerie
equalize	ermine	
equanimity	erode	
equate	eroneous	erroneous
equator	erosion	
equatorial	erotic	
equestrian	err (mistake, see	
equidistant	air, heir)	
equilateral	errand	
equilibrium	errant (traveling,	
equine	see arrant)	
equinoctial	erratic	
equinox	erratum	
equip	erroneous	
equitable	error	
equity	ersatz	
equivalent	erstwhile	
equivocal	erudite	

erupt		essential	
Eryan	Aryan	establish	
escalate		estate	
esay	essay	esteem	
escalator		esthetics/	
escapade		aesthetics	
escape		estimable	
escarole		estimate	
escarp		estop	
eschew		estoppage	
escort		estrange	
escrow		estrogen	
escue	eschew	estrus (or	
Esculous	Aeschylus	oestrus)	
escutcheon		estuary	
esel	easel	estute	astute
esence	essence	et cetera	
esential	essential	etching	
eshelon	echelon	eternal	
esop	Aesop	eternity	
esophagus		ether	
esoteric		ethereal	
Espagnole		ethical	
especially		ethics	
Esperanto		ethnic	
espionage		ethnocentrism	
esplanade		ethos	
espouse		ethyl	
espresso		etible	edible
esprit de corps		etiology	
espy		etiquette	
esquire		Etruscan	
essay (try, see		etude	
assay)		etymology	
essence		eucalyptus	

Eucharist		exact	
euchre		exaggerate	
eugenic		exalt (glorify,	
eulogy		see exult)	
eulogize		examine	
eunuch		examination	
euphemism		example	
euphonic		exasperate	
euphoria		excavate	
eureka		exceed (outdo,	
Eustachian tube		see accede)	
euthanasia		excel	
evacuate		excellent	
evade		excellerate	accelerate
evaluate		excelsior	
evanescent		excentric	eccentric
evangelical		except (exclude,	
evangelist		see accept)	
evaporate		excerpt	
evasion		excess (overage,	
eventide		see access)	
eventual		exchequer	
eventually		excise	
evesdrop	eavesdrop	excite	
evict		exclaim	
evidence		exclamation	
evidently		exclamatory	
evince		exclude	
eviscerate		exclusive	
evocation		excommunicate	
evocative		excoriate	
evoke		excrement	
evolution		excrescence	
evolve		excrete	
exacerbate		excretory	

excruciating
excursion
excusable
excuse
execrable
execute
executive
executrix
exegesis
exemplary
exemplify
exempt
exercise (activity,
  see (exorcise)
exert
exhalation
exhale
exhaust
exhibit
exhibitor
exhilarate
exhort
exhortation
exhume
exigency
exiguous
exile
exist
existence
existentialism
exodus
exonerate
exorable
exorbitant

exorcise (expell
  spirits, see
  exercise)
exotic
expand
expanse
expatriate
expectant
expectorate
expedient
expedite
expedition
expeditious
expel
expendable
expenditure
expense
experience
experiment
expert
expertise
expiate
expiration
explain
explanatory
expletive
explicable
explicatory
explicit
exploit
explore
explosion
exponent
export

expose
expose/exposé
exposition
ex post facto
expostulate
exposure
expound
express
expropriate
expulsion
expunge
expurgate
exquisite
extant (lasting,
  see extent)
extasy   ecstasy
extatic   ecstatic
extemporaneous
extemporize
extension
extensive
extent (size, see
  extant)
extenuate
exterior
exterminate
external
extinct
extinguish
extirpate
extol
extort

extract
extracurricular
extradite
extramarital
extraneous
extraordinary
extrapolate
extrasensory
  perception
extraterritorial
extravagance
extreme
extremist
extricable
extricate
extrinsic
extrovert
extrusion
exuberant
exude
exult (jubilant,
  see exalt)
exultation
exume   exhume
exzema   eczema
eye (vision,
  see aye)
eyelet (hole,
  see islet)
eyre (journey,
  see ire)

F

fabricate		falable	fallible
fabulous		falacious	fallacious
facade		falanx	phalanx
facet		falcon	
facetious		fallacious	
facile		fallacy	
facility		fallible	
facsimile		fallic	phallic
faction		Fallopian tube	
factory		fallow	
factorum		fallus	phallus
factsimile	facsimile	Falopian tube	Fallopian tube
factual		falow	fallow
faculty		falsetto	
faddist		falsify	
Fahrenheit		falsity	
failure		falter	
faint (pass out, see feint)		familiar	
		family	
fairy (pixie, see ferry)		famine	
		famish	
fait accompli		famous	
faker (one who fakes)		fanagle	finagle
		fanatic	
fakir (Hindu ascetic)		fandango	
		fanfare	

fantastic		feable	feeble
fantasy		feance	fiance/fiancé (male)
fantom	phantom		
farce			fiancee/fianceé (female)
farina			
Farisee	Pharisee		pheasant
farther (more distant, see further)		feasible	fiasco
		feat (deed, see feet)	
farynx	pharynx		
fasade	facade	feather	
fascetious	facetious	feckless	
fascinate		fecund	
fascism		fedelity	fidelity
faset	facet	fedora	
fasilitate	facilitate	feduciary	fiduciary
fasility	facility	feeble	
fasle	facile	feet (pl. foot, see feat)	
fasten			
fastidious		feign	
fatal		feind	fiend
fathom		feirce	fierce
fatigue		feint (trick, see faint)	
fatten			
fatuous		felicitate	
faucet		felicity	
fault		feline	
faun (deity, see fawn)		felon	
		felony	
fauna		feminine	
faux pas		femme fatale	
favorite		fennel	
fawn (deer, see faun)		fenobarbital	phenobarbital
		fenomenon	phenomenon
faze (disturb, see phase)		fenotype	phenotype
		feord	fjord

feott	fiat	fiddle	
feral		fidelity	
fer-de-lance		fidget	
ferlough	furlough	fiduciary	
ferment		fiend	
ferocious		fierce	
ferret		fiery	
ferrous		fiesta	
ferry (boat, see		fifth	
fairy)		fiftieth	
fertile		fifty	
fertilize		figet	fidget
fervent		figment	
fervid		figurine	
fervor		filabuster	filibuster
festival		filament	
festoon		filanderer	philanderer
fether	feather	filately	philately
fetid		filbert	
fetish		filch	
fetter		fileal	filial
fetus		filegree	filigree
feud		filial	
feudal (medieval,		filibuster	
see futile)		filigree	
fever		Filipino	
fiance/fiancé		fillament	filament
(male)		fillet	
fiancee/fianceé		filly	
(female)		filodendron	philodendron
fiasco		filogeny	phylogeny
fiat		filtch	filch
fibrillation		filter (strainer,	
fickle		see philter)	
fictitious		filthy	

finacky	finicky	flamboyant	
finagle		flamenco	
finale		flamingo	
finance		flammable	
financier		flapper	
finesse (trick, see finis)		flare (blaze, see flair)	
finicky		flattery	
finis (end, see finesse)		flaunt	
finish		flavor	
finite		flaxen	
finnig	phennig	flea (insect, see flee)	
fiord/fjord		fledgling	
fir (tree, see fur)		flee (run away, see flea)	
firmament		fleece	
fiscal (finance, see physical)		flegmatic	phlegmatic
fission		flem	phlegm
fissure		fleur-de-lis	
fistic		flew (did fly, see flu, flue)	
fisticuffs		flexible	
fixation		flimsy	
fizzle		flippant	
fjord/fiord		flirtation	
flabbergast		floage	flowage
flaccid		flocculate	
flack	flak	flogistic	phlogistic
flagellate		flogging	
flagon		floral	
flagrant		florescent	fluorescent
flair (insight, see flare)		floriculture	
flak		florid	
flamable	flammable	floridate	fluoridate

florinate	fluorinate	Foebe	Phoebe
floroscope	fluoroscope	fogy (person,	
flotation		see foggy)	
flotilla		foggy (weather,	
flotsam		see fogy)	
flounce		foible	
flounder		foier	foyer
flour (grain, see		foist	
flower)		folcrum	fulcrum
flowage		foleage	foliage
flower (blossom,		foliage	
see flour)		folio	
flu (influenza,		follicle	
see flew, flue)		folly	
fluctuate		folsetto	falsetto
flue (chimney,		foment	
see flew, flu)		fon	faun
fluent		fona	fauna
flugel horn/		fondant	
flügel horn		fondle	
fluid		fondue	
fluke		fonetic	phonetic
flummox		fo pa	faux pas
fluorescent		foppery	
fluoridate		forage	
fluorinate		foray	
fluoroscope		forceps	
flur-de-lee	fleur-de-lis	forcible	
flurry		forebear	
flute		foreclosure	
flutter		foreign	
fobia	phobia	forensic	
fobic	phobic	foreword	
focal		(preface, see	
focus		forward)	
fodder		forego	forgo

forfeit
forge
forgery
forgo
forlorn
formaldehyde
formally (cus-
  tom, see
  formerly)
format
formative
formerly (past,
  see formally)
formidable
formula
forrensic   forensic
fosphate   phosphate
fosphorescense   phosphor-
                     escence
forsythia
fort (stronghold)
forte (ability)
forth (forward,
  see fourth)
fortieth
fortify
fortissimo
fortitude
fortnight
fortress
fortuitous
fortunate
forty
forum
forward (near,
  see foreword)

fossil
foto   photo
foul (ugly, see
  fowl)
foundation
foundry
fountain
fourteen
fourth (after
  third, see
  forth)
fowl (bird, see
  foul)
foyer
fracas
fraction
fracture
fragile
fragment
fragrant
fraight   freight
frail
franchise
frankfurter
frankincense
frantic
frantically
frappe/frappé
fraternity
frau
fraud
fraught
fraulein/
  fraülein
freakish
freedom

freeze (cold,
  see frieze)
frehol   frijole
freight
frenetic/phrenetic
frenology   phrenology
frenzy
frequent
fresco
Freudian
freülein   fraulein/
               fraülein
friar (clergy, see
  fryer)
fricassee
friend
frieze (orna-
  ment, see
  freeze)
frigate
frigid
frijole
fringe
frippery
frisky
fritter
frivolous
frolic
frontier
frontispiece
frothy
frugal
fruition
frustrate
fryer (chicken,
  see friar)

fuchsia
fudal   feudal
fude   feud
fuehrer
fugitive
fugue
fulcrum
fulfill
fulsome
fumigate
fundamental
funeral
funeral (service)
funereal (sad)
funnel
fur (animal skin,
  see fir)
furl
furlough
furnace
furer   fuehrer
furniture
furor
furrow
further (in addi-
  tion, see
  farther)
furtive
fuse
fuselage
fushia   fuchsia
fusible
fusillade
futile (useless,
  see feudal)
futurity

G

gabardine (coat)
gaberdine
  (fabric)
gadfly
gadget
gage (pledge, see
  gauge)
gaget   gadget
gaiety/gayety
gait (way of
  walking, see
  gate)
galaxy
Galic   Gaelic
gallant
galleon
gallery
galley
gallop
galore
galosh
galvanize
gama   gamma
gambit
gamble (to bet)
gambol (play)

gamma
gamut
gangling
ganglion
gangrene
garage
garbage
gard   guard
gardenia
gardian   guardian
garelous   garrulous
gargantuan
gargoyle
garish
garlic
garnishee
garrison
garrulous
gaseous
gasket
gastly   ghastly
gastric
gastronomy
gate (opening,
  see gait)
gauche

gaudy		gentleman	
gauge (measure,		gentry	
see gage)		genuflect	
gaunt		genuine	
gauntlet		genus	
gauze		geodesic	
gavel		geodetic	
gawk		geography	
gayety/gaiety		geology	
gazebo		geometry	
gazelle		geophysics	
gazette		geopolitical	
Geiger counter		geraffe	giraffe
geiser	geyser	geranium	
geisha		gerend	gerund
gelatin		gergle	gurgle
gendarme		geriatrics	
gene (heredity,		gerkin	gherkin
see jean)		germane	
geneal	genial	germicide	
genealogy		germinal	
generate		germination	
generic		gerrymander	
generous		Gerter	Goethe
genesis		gerund	
genetics		gesha	geisha
genial		gest/geste	
genital		(adventure,	
genitive		see jest)	
genius		gestation	
genocide		gesticulate	
genre		gesture	
genteel		gesundheit	
gentian		geyser	
gentile		ghastly	
gentility		gherkin	

ghetto		gizzard	
ghoulish		glacier	
giant		gladiator	
gibberish		gladiola	
gibbon		glamour	
gibe/jibe		glandular	
giblet		glib	
gigantic		glicerin	glycerin
giger counter	Geiger counter	glimmer	
gigolo		glimpse	
gila monster		glisten	
gild (gold		gloat	
covered, see		global	
guild)		globular	
gile	guile	gloomy	
gillotine	guillotine	glorify	
gilt (gold-		glorious	
colored, see		glossary	
guilt)		glossy	
gimmick		glote	gloat
gingham		glucose	
gingivitis		glutton	
ginny pig	guinea pig	glycerin	
ginocology	gynecology	gnarl	
ginrikisha	jinrikisha	gnash	
gip	gyp	gnat	
gipsum	gypsum	gnaw	
gipsy/gypsy		gnome	
giraffe		gnu (animal, see	
girate	gyrate	knew, new)	
girder		goad	
girdle		gobbledygook	
girth		goblet	
giser	geyser	goblin	
gist		goerd	gourd
gitar	guitar	Goethe	

gofer	gopher	granade	grenade
goggles		granary	
goiter		grandeur	
golf (game, see		grandiloquence	
gulf)		grandiose	
golosh	galosh	granite	
gondola		granular	
gonorrhea		granulate	
gopher		graphic	
gorgeous		graphite	
gormet	gourmet	grapple	
gorilla (ape, see		grate (fireplace,	
guerrilla)		see great)	
goshe	gauche	gratify	
gossamer		gratitude	
gossip		gratuity	
gouge		gratuitous	
goulash		gravity	
goulish	ghoulish	grayhound	greyhound
gourd		great (large, see	
gourmet		grate)	
gout		greed	
governable		greet	
government		gregarious	
governor		greive	grieve
gown		greivence	grievance
gracious		gremlin	
gradation		grenade	
gradient		grenadier	
gradual		grenadine	
graduate		greyhound	
grafite	graphite	gridiron	
gragarious	gregarious	grievance	
grain		grieve	
grainary	granary	grievous	
grammar		grill	

grimace
grime
grip (clutch)
grippe (infection)
grisly (horrible,
    see grizzly)
gristle
grizzly (bear, see
    grisly)
groan (moan, see
    grown)
groggy
grommet
grosgrain ribbon
grotesque
grotto
grouchy
grouse
grovel
grown (mature,
    see groan)
grudge
gruel
gruesome
grumble
guarantee (agree-
    ment)
guaranty (war-
    rant)
guard
guardian
gubernatorial
guerrilla (soldier,
    see gorilla)

guffaw
guidance
guide
guild (associa-
    tion, see gild)
guile
guillotine
guilt
guinea pig
guise (false man-
    ners, see guys)
guitar
gulf (chasm, see
    golf)
gullible
gully
gulosh　　　　goulash
gumbo
gurgle
gutteral
guys (pl. men or
    ropes, see
    guise)
guzzle
gymnasium
gymnast
gynecology
gyp
gypsum
gypsy/gipsy
gyrate
gyration
gyroscope

H

habatat	habitat
habeas corpus	
haberdashery	
habitat	
habitual	
habitué	
hacienda	
hackneyed	
haddock	
Hagalian	Hegelian
haggard	
haggle	
hail (ice lumps, see hale)	
hair (fur, see hare)	
hairbrain	harebrain
hairy-kary	hara-kiri
halatosis	halitosis
halcyon	
hale (sound, see hail)	
halibut	
halitosis	
hallelujah	

halliard/halyard	
Halloween	
hallowed	
hallucination	
hallucinogen	
halseon	halcyon
halve	
halyard/halliard	
hamburger	
hammer	
hammock (suspended bed, see hummock)	
hamper	
handicap	
handicraft	
handkerchief	
handle	
handsome (suitable, see hansom)	
handy	
hangar (plane port)	

hanger (wire
  device)
hanker
hankerchief   handkerchief
hansom (cab, see
  handsome)
Hanukkah/
  Chanukah
hanous   heinous
haphazard
happy
hara-kiri
harangue
harass
harbinger
harbor
hardy
hare (rabbit, see
  hair)
harebrain
harem
hari-kiri   hara-kiri
harken/hearken
harlot
harmonica
harmonious
harmony
harness
harpoon
harpsichord
harrowing
harry
hart (stag, see
  heart)
harth   hearth
hartily   heartily

hary-kary   hara-kiri
harvester
hasenpfeffer
hashish
hassock
hatchet
hatred
haughty
haul
haunch
haunt
haven
haversack
havoc
hawthorn
hazardous
haze
hazelnut
heal (cure, see
  heel)
healthful
hear (heed, see
  here)
hearken/harken
hearse
heart (organ, see
  hart)
hearth
heartily
heat
heath
heathen
heather
heave
heaven
heavy

hebephrenia
heckle
hectic
hectograph
hedge
hedgemony   hegemony
hedonism
heed
heel (base, see
  heal)
heeth   heath
hefty
Hegelian
heffer   heifer
hege   hedge
hegemony
heifer
height
heinous
heir (inheritor,
  see air, err)
heist
heleum   helium
helical
helicopter
heliotrope
heliport
helium
helm
helmet
helter-skelter
hematology
hemisphere
hemlock
hemoglobin
hemophilia

hemorrhage
hemorrhoid
hemrige   hemorrhage
hemroid   hemorrhoid
henceforth
henna
hepatitis
herald
heraldic
herange   harangue
heratage   heritage
herb
herbaceous
herbivorous
herculean
here (now, see
  hear)
heredity
Hereford
herem   harem
heresy
heretic
Herford   Hereford
heringbone   herringbone
herisy   heresy
heritage
heritic   heretic
hermaphrodite
hermetic
hermit
hernia
heroin (drug)
heroine (female,
  hero)
herold   herald
heron

herredity	heredity	hindrance	
herringbone		hinge	
herse	hearse	hiphalutin	highfalutin
hesitate		hipnosis	hypnosis
heterodox		Hippocratic	
heterogeneous		oath	
heteronym		hippodrome	
heterosexual		hippopotamus	
heuristic		hire (employ,	
heven	heaven	see higher)	
hew (cut, see		hiroglyphic	hieroglyphic
hue)		hist	heist
hexagon		histamine	
hexameter		histology	
hiacinth	hyacinth	histrionic	
hiatus		hitherto	
hibachi		hives	
hibernate		hoar (frost, see	
hibiscus		whore)	
hibochi	hibachi	hoard (save, see	
hibred	hybrid	horde)	
hiccough/		hoarse (rough,	
hiccup		see horse)	
hideous		hoax	
hidrolic	hydraulic	hobble	
hidrangea	hydrangea	hobgoblin	
hierarchy		hockey	
hieroglyphic		hocus-pocus	
higher (taller, see		hodgepodge	
hire)		hoe	
highfalutin		hoi polloi	
hijack		hoist	
hilarious		hole (cavity, see	
him (pronoun,		whole)	
see hymn)		holigan	hooligan
himan	hymen	holiness	

hollandaise		horendous	horrendous
hollow		horible	horrible
holocaust		horid	horrid
holster		horizontal	
holyness	holiness	hormone	
homage		hornet	
homacide	homicide	horoscope	
homaletic	homiletic	horrendous	
homany grits	hominy grits	horrible	
homely		horrid	
homeopath		horror	
homicide		hors d'oeuvre	
homiletic		horse (animal,	
homily		see hoarse)	
hominy grits		horticulture	
homogeneous		hosiery	
homogenize		hospital	
homologous		hostage	
homonym		hostel (housing)	
homosexual		hostile (un-	
Honakah	Hanukkah/	friendly)	
	Chanukah	hovel	
honesty		hover	
honky		howitzer	
honor		howl	
honorarium		hoy paloi	hoi polloi
hooch		hubbub	
hoodlum		huch	hooch
hooligan		huckleberry	
hootenanny		huckster	
hoping (wishing)		hue (color, see	
hopping		hew)	
(jumping)		huge	
horascope	horoscope	hullabaloo	
horde (crowd,		humador	humidor
see hoard)		humanitarian	

humble		hydrangea	
humerus (arm-		hydrant	
bone, see		hydrate	
humorous)		hydraulic	
humid		hydrocarbon	
humidor		hydrochloric	
humiliate		hydrodynamics	
humility		hydroelectric	
humis	humus	hydrogen	
hummock/		hydrogenate	
hammock		hydrolic	hydraulic
humor		hydrolysis	
humoresque		hydrometer	
humorous		hydrophobia	
(funny, see		hydrotherapy	
humerus)		hydroxide	
humus		hyfen	hyphen
hundred		hygiene	
hundredth		hymen	
hunger		hymn (song,	
hunta	junta	see him)	
hurbaceous	herbaceous	hyperbola (math)	
hurbivorous	herbivorous	hyperbole	
hurdle (barrier,		(overstate)	
see hurtle)		hyphen	
hurdy-gurdy		hypnosis	
hurl		hypnotize	
hurmophrodite	hermaphrodite	hypochondria	
hurricane		hypocrisy	
hurried		hypocrite	
hurtle (collide,		hypodermic	
see hurdle)		hypotension	
husky		hypotenuse	
hustings		hypothalamus	
hustle		hypothesis	
hyacinth		hypothesize	
hybrid		hypothetical	

hyssop   hysteria
hysterectomy

I

iambic
ibidem (ibid.)
ibis
ichthyology
icicle
icing
icon/ikon
iconoclast
iconography
ictheology   ichthyology
icumenical   ecumenical
icycle   icicle
ideal
idel   idle
identical
identify
ideology
iderdown   eiderdown
idiocy
idiom
idiomatic
idiosyncrasy
idiot
idle (useless)
idol (statue)

idolater
idolatry
idolize
idyl/idyll (poem)
igloo
igneous
ignite
ignition
ignoble
ignominious
ignoramous
ignorance
ignore
iguana
ikon/ icon
I'll (I will; see
    aisle, isle)
illegal
illegible
illegitimate
illiberal
illicit (unlawful,
    see elicit)
illimitable
illiteracy

illogical
illuminate
illusion (false
  idea, see
  allusion)
illusory
illustrate
illustrator
illustrious
ilucidate   elucidate
image
imagery
imagine
imbalance
imbalm   embalm
imbecile
imbed   embed
imbibe
imbitter   embitter
imboss   emboss
imbroglio
imbue
imitate
immaculate
immanent (in-
  dwelling, see
  eminent; immi-
  nent)
immaterial
immature
immeasurable
immediate
immemorial
immense
immerse

immersion (in
  water, see
  emersion)
inmesh/enmesh
immigrate (move
  into, see
  emigrate)
imminent (im-
  pending, see
  eminent,
  immanent)
immobile
immoderate
immodest
immolate
immoral
immortal
immune
immutable
impacted
impairment
impale
impalpable
impartial
impasse
impassioned
impassive
impatient
impeach
impeccable
impecunious
impede
impediment
impel
impend

impenetrable   import
impenitence   importable
imperative   importance
imperceptible   importunate
imperceptive   importune
imperfect   impose
imperial   imposition
imperious   impossible
imperishable   impostor
impermanent   imposture
impermeable   impotent
impersonal   impound
impersonate   impoverish
impertinence   impractical
imperturbable   imprasario   impresario
impervious   imprecate
impetigo   imprecise
impetuous   impregnable
impetus   impregnate
impiety   impresario
impinge   impress
impious   imprimatur
impish   imprint
implacable   imprison
implacement   emplacement   improbable
implant   impromptu
implausible   improper
implement   impropriety
implicate   improvident
implicit   improvise
implore   imprudent
imply   impugn
impolite   impulse
impolitic   impunity
imponderable   impute

imune	immune	incautious	
in absentia		incendiary	
inaccessible		incense	
inaccuracy		incentive	
inadequate		incephalitis	encephalitis
inadmissible		inception	
inadvertent		incessant	
inadvisable		incestuous	
inalienable		inchoate	
inalterable		inchant	enchant
inamorata		incident	
inane		incidious	insidious
inanimate		incindiary	incendiary
inappeasable		incinerate	
inapplicable		incipid	insipid
inappreciable		incipience (early	
inapproachable		stage, see in-	
inards	innards	sipience)	
inarticulate		incipient	
inartistic		incircle	encircle
inate	innate	incise	
inattentive		incision	
inaudible		incisive	
inaugural		incisor	
inaugurate		incite (instigate,	
inauspicious		see insight)	
inbed	embed	inclement	
incalculable		inclose/enclose	
incamptment	encampment	incognito	
incandescent		incoherent	
incantation		incombustible	
incapable		incommensurate	
incapacitate		incommodious	
incarcerate		incommunicable	
incarnate		incommunicado	

incomparable	incumber	encumber
incompass	encompass	incur	
incompatible	incurable	
incompetence	indebted	
incompliant	indecency	
incomprehensible	indecipherable	
inconceivable	indecision •	
inconclusive	indecisive	
incongruous	indecorum	
inconsequential	indefatigable	
inconsistent	indefeasible	
inconsolable	indefenite	indefinite
inconsonant	indefensible	
inconspicuous	indefinable	
inconstant	indefinite	
incontestable	indegent	indigent
incontinent	indego	indigo
incontrovertible	indelible	
inconvenient	indelicate	
incorporate	indemnify	
incorrect ·	indemnity	
incorrigible	indentation	
incorruptible	indenture	
increase	independence	
incredible	indescernible	indiscernible
incredulous	indescreet	indiscreet
increment	indescretion	indiscretion
incriminate	indescribable	
incrustation	indespensable	indispensable
incubate	indestructible	
incubator	indeterminate	
incubus	indicate	
inculcate	indict (accuse,	
inculpate	see indite)	
incumbent	indifference	

indigenous
indigent
indigestion
indignant
indigo
indiscernible
indiscreet
indiscretion
indiscribable   indescribable
indiscriminate
indispensable
indisposed
indisputable
indissoluble
indistinct
indistinguishable
indistructible   indestructible
indite (enjoin,
  see indict)
individual
indivisible
indoctrinate
indolent
indomitable
indubitable
induce
induct
indue/endue
indulge
indulgent
industrialist
industrious
inebriate
inedible
ineffable

ineffaceable
ineffective
ineffectual
inefficacious
inefficient
inelastic
inelegance
ineligible
ineluctable
inept
ineptitude
inequality
inequitable
inequity (injus-
  tice, see
  iniquity)
ineradicable
inerasable
inert
inertia
inervate   innervate
inescapable
inessential
inestimable
inevitable
inexcusable
inexhaustible
inexorable
inexpedient
inexpensive
inexperience
inexplicable
inexpressible
inextricable
infadel   infidel

infadelity   infidelity   infraction
infallible   infrared
infamous   infrequent
infant   infringe
infantesimal infinitesimal infuriate
infanticide   infuse
infantile   infusion
infantry   ingenious
infared   infrared   (clever, see
infatuate   ingenuous)
infection   ingenue/ingénue
inferior   ingenuity
infernal   ingenuous (inno-
inferno   cent, see
infidel   ingenious)
infidelity   ingest
infiltrate   Inglish   English
infinite   inglorious
infinitesimal   ingot
infinitive   ingraciate   ingratiate
infinity   ingrained
infirmary   ingrate
infirmity   ingratiate
inflammable   ingredient
inflammation   ingress
inflate   ingross   engross
inflation   inhabit
inflection   inhabitable
inflexible   inhabitant
inflict   inhalation
influence   inhale
influenza   inhance   enhance
influx   inharmonious
informal   inherent
informer   inherit

inhesion		innimical	inimical
inhibit		innimitable	inimitable
inhibitor		inning	
inhospitable		innocent	
inhumane		innoculate	inoculate
inhume		innocuous	
iniciate	initiate	innovate	
iniciative	initiative	innovator	
inimical		innuendo	
inimitable		innumerable	
ining	inning	inoculate	
iniquity		inoffensive	
(wickedness,		inofficious	
see inequity)		inoperable	
initial		inoperative	
initiate		inopportune	
initiative		inordinate	
inject		inorganic	
injest	ingest	inovate	innovate
injoin	enjoin	inquisition	
injudicious		inquisitive	
injunction		inquisitor	
injure		insaciable	insatiable
injurious		insalar	insular
injustice		insalate	insulate
inkling		insalater	insulator
in memorium		insalin	insulin
inmesh	enmesh	insane	
inequity	iniquity	insanity	
innards		insatiable	
innate		inscrutable	
innebriate	inebriate	inseceptible	insusceptible
innertia	inertia	insecticide	
innervate		insecure	
(nerves, see		inselin	insulin
enervate)		insemination	

insensate
insense   incense
insensible
insensitive
inseparable
insephalitis   encephalitis
insert
insidious
insight (percep-
   tion, see
   incite)
insignia
insignificant
insincere
insinuate
insipid
insipience (lack
   of wisdom, see
   incipience)
insirgent   insurgent
insirmountable   insurmount-
                             able
insirrection   insurrection
insistence
insite   incite
insize   incize
insolation
insole
insolent
insoluble
insolvable
insolvency
insomnia
insomniac
insouciance
inspect

inspector
inspirational
inspirit
instability
install
installation
instant
instantaneous
instead
instigate
instigator
instinct
institute
instruct
instrument
insubordinate
insubstantial
insuceiance   insouciance
insufferable
insufficient
insular
insulate
insulin
insuperable
insupportable
insurance
insurgent
insurmountable
insurrection
insusceptible
intact
intager   integer
intangible
integer
integral
integrate

integrity

intellect

intelligent

intelligentsia

intelligible

intemperate

intend

intense

inter

intercede

intercept

intercession

intercom

intercourse

interdependence

interdict

interest

interfere

interference

interim

interior

interlace

interlinear

interlining

interlocutor

interloper

intermarriage

intermediary

intermediate

intermezzo

interminable

intermission

intermittent

intermural (be-

  tween walls, see

  intramural)

intern/interne

internecine

interogate   interrogate

interpolate

interpose

interpret

interregnum

interrogate

interrupt

intersect

intersperse

interstate

  (between states,

  see intrastate)

interstellar

interstice

interum   interim

interval

intervene

intervenous   intravenous

interweave

intestate

intestine

intimate

intimidate

intolerable

intolerant

intonation

intoxicant

intoxicate

intractable

intramural

  (sports, see in-

  termural)

intransigent

intransitive

intrastate (within a state, see interstate)		invidious	
		invigorating	
		invincible	
intravenous		inviolable	
intrepid		inviolate	
intricacy		invisible	
intricate		invision	envision
intrigue		invitation	
intrinsic		invocation	
introit		invoice	
introjection		invoke	
introspective		involuntary	
introversion		involution	
introvert		involve	
intuition		invulnerable	
intuitive		inward	
inundate		ioda	iota
invagle	inveigle	iodide	
invalid		iodine	
invaluable		ion	
invariable		ionosphere	
invasion		iota	
invay	inveigh	irascible	
invective		irate	
inveigh		ire (anger, see eyre)	
inveigle			
inuendo	innuendo	iridescent	
inventory		iris	
inveriable	invariable	irksome	
inverse		irony	
inversion		irradescent	iridescent
invertebrate		irradiate	
investigator		irrascible	irascible
investiture		irrational	
investor		irreclaimable	
inveterate		irreconcilable	

irrecoverable
irredeemable
irreducible
irrefutable
irregular
irrelevant
irreligious
irremediable
irreparable
irreplacable
irrepressible
irreproachable
irresistible
irresolute
irrespective
irresponsible
irretrievable
irreverence
irreversible
irrevocable
irrigate
irritable
irritant
irritate

irruption
isinglass
island
isle (small island,
    see aisle, I'll)
islet (small is-
    land, see eyelet)
ismus   isthmus
isobar
isolate
isosceles
isotope
issue
issuing
isthmus
italic
itemize
itinerant
itinerary
its (possessive)
it's (it is)
ivory
ivy

J

jackal		jeopardy	
jacket		jepardy	jeopardy
jagged		jerkin (jacket,	
jaguar		see gherkin)	
Jahovah	Jehovah	jerrymander	gerrymander
jajune	jejune	jersey	
jalopy		jest (mock,	
Jambalaya		see gest)	
jamboree		jesture	gesture
janitor		jettison	
jargon		jetty	
jasmine		jewel	
jaundice		jewlery	jewelry
jaunty		jibe/gibe	
javelin		jigger	
jazmine	jasmine	jiggle	
jealousy		jingo	
jean (pants,		jinks	
see gene)		jinrikisha	
jeep		jitney	
jejune		jockey	
jelatin	gelatin	jocose	
jelopy	jalopy	jocular	
jelousy	jealousy	jocund	

jodhpurs		juggler	
joggle		jugular vein	
joie de vivre		jujitsu	
jollity		julep	
jondarm	gendarme	julienne	
jonquil		Jumbolaya	Jambalaya
jonre	genre	junction	
jostle		juncture	
journal		jungle	
journey		junior	
joust		juniper	
jovial		junket	
jowl		junta	
juah de veeve	joie de vivre	juridical	
jubilant		jurisdiction	
jubilation		jurisprudence	
jubilee		jurney	journey
judge		jurnal	journal
judicate		juror	
judicial		justice	
judiciary		justification	
judicious		juvenile	
juditsu	jujitsu	juxtapose	
juggernaut		juxtaposition	

K

kabal	cabal	kelp	
kaiak	kayak	kemona	kimono
kaiser		kenetic	kinetic
kaki	khaki	kennel	
kale		kerchief	
kaleidoscope		kernel (seed,	
kamikaze		see colonel)	
kangaroo		keropody	chiropody
kanto	canto	kerosene	
kaos	chaos	ketchup/catsup	
kapok		key (lock, see	
kapon	capon	quay)	
kaput		khaki	
karakul		kibitzer	
karat (gold, see		kidnap	
carat, caret,		kidney	
carrot)		kiln	
karisma	charisma	kilocycle	
kason	caisson	kilometer	
katsup	ketchup	kilowatt	
katydid		kimono	
kayak		kindergarten	
keask	kiosk	kindle	
keenness		kindred	

kinescope		knob	
kinesthetic		knockwurst	
kinetic		knoll	
kiosk		knot (tied rope,	
kiote	coyote	see not)	
kirsch		knowledge	
kiser	kaiser	knowledgeable	
kismet		knuckle	
kitchenette		koala	
kitty-corner/		Kodiak bear	
cater-corner		kohlrabi	
kleptomaniac		komikaze	kamikaze
knack		Koran	
knapsack		kosher	
knave (rogue,		kowtow	
see nave)		kripton	krypton
knead (mix, see		Kremlin	
need)		krone (coin, see	
knee		crone)	
kneel		kroquet	croquet
knell		krypton	
knew (to know,		kudos	
see gnu, new)		kulottes	culottes
knickers		kumin	cumin
knickknack/		kumquat	
nicknack			
knight (soldier,			
see night)			

L

labatory	laboratory	laden	
laberinth	labyrinth	lading	
labidinal	libidinal	ladle	
laborer		lager beer	
laboratory		laggard	
laborious		lagistics	logistics
labotomy	lobotomy	lagitimate	legitimate
labretto	libretto	lagoon	
labyrinth		laison	liaison
lacerate		laissez faire	
lachrymal		laity	
lachrymose		lama (monk, see	
lackadaisical		llama)	
lackey		lamanar	laminar
laconic		lamanate	laminate
lacquer		lamb	
lacrimal	lachrymal	lambaste	
lacrimose	lachrymose	lame/lamé	
lacrosse		lament	
lactation		laminar	
lactic acid		laminate	
lactose		lampion	
lacuna		lampoon	
ladder (steps,		lamprey eel	
see latter)		lancet	

landau		lathe (machine)	
language		latice	lattice
languid		latitude	
languish		latrine	
languor		latter (last, see	
lanoleum	linoleum	ladder)	
lanolin		lattice	
lanset	lancet	laturgical	liturgical
lantern		laud	
lanyard		laudanum	
lapel		laudatory	
lapidary		laugh	
lapse		launch	
laquer	lacquer	launder	
larceny		laureate	
larder		laurel	
lareat	lariat	lavaliere	
larengitis	laryngitis	lavatory	
largess		lavender	
larghetto		lavish	
largo		lawd	laud
lariat		lawdanum	laudanum
larseny	larceny	lawdatory	laudatory
larva		lawn	
laryngitis		lawyer	
larynx		laxative	
lasagna		laxity	
lascerate	lacerate	layette	
lascivious		layman	
lassitude		lazafaire	laissez faire
lasso		lazanya	lasagna
lateen sail		lazaretto	
latent		leach (to remove,	
lateral		see leech)	
latex		lead (guide or	
lath (fiberboards)		metal)	

leader		legal	
league		legate	
leak (slow loss, see leek)		legation	
		legato	
lean (incline, see lien)		leger	ledger
		legend	
lear	leer	legendary	
leash		legerdemain	
least		leget	legate
leasure	leisure	leggacy	legacy
leatard	leotard	leggings	
leather		legible	
leaven		legion	
lebedinal	libidinal	legionnaire	
Leberstraum	Lieberstraum	legislate	
lecher		legislature	
lecherous		legitimate	
leconic	laconic	legitimacy	
lectern		legon	legion
lecture		legonaire	legionnaire
led (past tense of lead)		legue	league
		legume	
leder	liter	leisure	
ledge		leitmotiv	
ledger		lemma	
leech (blood sucker, see leach)		lemming	
		lemur	
leek (herb, see leak)		length	
		lenient	
leer		lenity	
leery		lentil (plant, see lintel)	
leeward		leopard	
leeway		leotard	
legable	legible	lepard	leopard
legacy		leper	

lepersy	leprosy	lewd	
lepidopterous		lexicography	
leprechaun		lexicon	
leprosy		liable (responsibil-	
Lesbian		ity, see libel)	
lesion		liaison	
lesiveous	lascivious	liar (falsifier, see	
lessee		lyre)	
lesson		libary	library
lessor		libation	
letcher	lecher	libedinal	libidinal
letcherous	lecherous	libel (false state-	
leter	liter	ment, see liable)	
lether	leather	liberal	
lethal		liberate	
lethargic		libertarian	
lethargy		libertine	
lettuce		libidinal	
leucite (silicate,		libido	
see Lucite)		library	
leucocyte/leuko-		librarian	
cyte		libretto	
leukemia		librium	
leukocyte/leuco-		lice	
cyte		license	
levée (embank-		licentious	
ment, see levy)		liceum	lyceum
leven	leaven	lichen (plant, see	
leviathan		liken)	
levity		licit	
levy (tax, see		licorice	
levee)		lie (untruth, see	
lew	lieu	lye)	
leward	leeward	Lieberstraum	
leway	leeway	liege	

lien (legal, see lean)		lineal	
lienent	lenient	lineament	
lieu		linear	
lieutenant		lineate	
ligament		linen	
ligature		Lineotype	Linotype
lightening (brightening)		lingerie	
lightning (electricity)		linguist	
likelihood		liniment	
liken (compare, see lichen)		linoleum	
lilac		Linotype	
lile	lisle	lintel (above door, see lentil)	
Lilliputian		linx	lynx
lily		lionize	
limb (appendage, see limn)		lionnaise	lyonnaise
limber		liquefaction	
limbo		liquefy	
limelight		liqueur	
limerick		liquidate	
limit		liquor	
limn (draw, see limb)		lisence	license
limousine		lisentious	licentious
limph	lymph	lisine	lysine
limphatic	lymphatic	lisis	lysis
limpid		lisit	licit
Limrick	Limerick	lisivious	lascivious
linage/lineage		lisle	
linament	liniment	lissome	
linch	lynch	listen	
		litany	
		litegate	litigate
		liter	
		literacy	
		literal	

literature		lodge	
litergy	liturgy	loganberry	
lithe		logarithm	
lithograph		loger beer	lager beer
litigate		logical	
litmotif	leitmotiv	logistics	
litmus paper		logy	
littany	litany	loincloth	
litter		loiter	
liturgical		loneliness	
liturgy		lonely	
livelihood		longerie	lingerie
liver		longevity	
liverwurst		longitude	
livery		loom	
livid		loose	
lizard		lopsided	
llama (animal, see lama)		loquacious	
		lore	
loadstar/lodestar		Lorelei	
loadstone/lode-stone		lorengitis	laryngitis
loam		lose (verb, see loss)	
loathe		losenger	lozenge
lobe		loss (noun, see lose)	
loblolly pine		lothe	loath
lobotomy		lotion	
lobster		lottery	
lobule		lotus	
locket		lounge	
locomotion		louse	
locust		loutish	
locution		louver	
lodestar/loadstar		lovable	
lodestone/load-stone		lovaliere	lavaliere

lozenge
lubricate
lucid
Lucite (plastic,
    see leucite)
lucocyte   leucocyte
lucrative
lucre
ludicrous
luftwaffe
luggage
lugubrious
lukemia   leukemia
lull
lullaby
lumbago
lumbar (vertebra)
lumber (wood)
luminary
luminescent
luminous
lummox
lunacy
lunar
lunatic
luncheon
luncheonette
lunge

lurch
lurid
lurk
luscious
lustrous
lutenant   lieutenant
Lutheran
luver   louver
luxuriant
luxuriate
luxurious
luxury
lyceum
lye (soap, see
    lie)
lymph
lymphatic
lynch
lynx
lyonnaise
lyre (harp, see
    liar)
lyric
lysergic acid di-
    ethylamide
lysine
lysis

M

ma'am
macabre
macadam
macaroni
macaroon
macaw
macerel   mackerel
machete
machination
machine
machinery
machinist
mackerel
macrocosm
macron
Macurochrome   Mercuro-
                   chrome
madam (English)
madame (French)
Madeira wine
mademoiselle
madonna
madras
madrigal
Madusa   Medusa

maelstrom
maestoso
maestro
magazine
magenta
maggot
magistrate
magna cum laude
magnafy   magnify
magnanimous
magnate (wealthy
   person, see mag-
   net)
magnatude   magnitude
magnesia
magnesium
magnet (lode-
   stone, see mag-
   nate)
magnificent
magnify
magnitude
magnolia
magot   maggot
maharaja

mahatma		maleria	malaria
Mah-Jongg		malestrom	maelstrom
mahogany		malevolent	
maiden		malfeasance	
mail (postal,		malformation	
see male)		malice	
maillot		malicious	
maim		malign	
main (principal,		malignant	
see mane)		maline	malign
maintain		malinger	
maître d'		malingerer	
maître d'hôtel		malisious	malicious
maize (corn, see		mall (promenade,	
maze)		see maul)	
majenta	magenta	mallard	
majesty		malleable	
Majong	Mah-Jong	maller	mauler
majority		mallet	
maladjusted		mallis	malice
malady		malmsey wine	
malaise		malnutrition	
malange	melange/	malot	mallet
	mélange	malpractice	
malaria		malstrom	maelstrom
malard	mallard	malt	
malatto	mulatto	maltase (enzyme)	
malay	melee	Maltese (language)	
malcontent		maltose (chemi-	
mal de mer		cal)	
male (mascu-		mam	ma'am
line, see mail)		mame	maim
maleable	malleable	mamen	mammon
maledy	malady	mammal	
malefactor		Mammalia	
malekite	malachite	mammary	

mammilla		manicle	manacle
mammon		manicure	
mammoth		manifest	
mamsey wine	malmsey wine	manifesto	
		manifold	
mana	manna	manipulate	
manafold	manifold	manna	
managerie	menagerie	mannaise	mayonnaise
mana ray	manta ray	mannequin	
manacle		manner (mode)	
manage		manor (mansion)	
manakin	mannequin	mansion	
mañana		manta ray	
manatee		manteia	mantilla
mandamus (writ of)		mantel (shelf, see mantle)	
mandarin		mantilla	
mandate		mantle (cloak, see mantel)	
mandatory			
mandible		manual	
mandolin		manufacture	
mane (hair, see main)		manure	
		manuscript	
maneac	maniac	manuver	maneuver
manefest	manifest	manyana	mañana
manefesto	manifesto	marabou	
manetee	manatee	maraca	
maneuver		maragold	marigold
manganate		maranade	marinade
mangle		maranate	marinate
mango		maraschino cherry	
mangy		marathon	
mania		marauder	
maniac		marawana	marijuana
manic			

Mardi gras		marshmallow	
mare		marsupial	
margarine		marten (animal,	
margin		see martin)	
marginal		marter	martyr
maridian	meridian	marterdom	martyrdom
marigold		martial (warlike,	
marijuana		see marshall)	
marimba		martin (bird, see	
marinade		marten)	
marinate		martinet	
marine		martyr	
marionette		martyrdom	
marital		marvel	
maritime		marvelous	
marjoram		marzipan	
markee	marquee	masa	mesa
marl		masacer	massacre
marlin		masacism	masochism
marmalade		mascara	
marmoset		mascerade	masquerade
marmot		mascot	
maroca	maraca	masculine	
maroon		maseur	masseur
marow	marrow	mashanation	machination
marquee (at a		Masiah	Messiah
theater)		masochism	
marquis (royalty)		masochist	
marquisette		mason	
marriage		masquerade	
marriageable		massacre	
marrow		massage	
marry		masseur	
marshal (official,		masseuse	
see martial)		massive	

mastadon   mastodon   mauve
masthead   maverick
masticate   mawkish
mastiff   maxim
mastodon   maximal
mastoid   maximum
masuse   masseuse   mayhem
matador   mayonnaise
maten   matin   mayor
matenee   matinee   maze (labyrinth,
mater de   maitre d´   see maize)
material (matter)   mazurka
materiel/matériel   M.C./emcee
   (equipment)   mead
maternal   meadow
maternity   meager
mathematics   mean (intend or
Mathuselah   Methuselah   middle, see
maticulous   meticulous   mein)
matier   metier/métier   meander
matin   meant
matinee   measles
matriarch   measure
matriculate   meat (food, see
matrimony   meet, mete)
matrix   mecca
matron   mechanic
matter   mechanism
mattress   medaphor   metaphor
Maudigra   Mardi gras   medal (award, see
mature   metal, mettle)
maudlin   medatarsal   metatarsal
maul (beat, see   meddle (interfere,
   mall)   see medal,
mauler   mettle)
mausoleum   medeocer   mediocre

medeocrity   mediocrity   melody
medetate   meditate   melon
media   membrane
median   memento
mediate   memoir
medical   memorabilia
medicate   memorable
medicinal   memorandum
medicine   memorial
medieval   memory
mediocre   menace
mediocrity   menage
meditate   menagerie
medium   mendacious
medley   mendicant
medow   meadow   menial
meek   meningitis
meerschaum   menopause
meet (contact,   menorah
  see meat, mete)   menstruate
megacycle   menstruation
megalomania   mensuration
megaphone   mental
megaton   menthol
meger   meager   mention
melancholia   mentor
melancholy   merange   meringue
melange/mélange   mercantile
melct   mulct   mercenary
melee   mercerized thread
meleu   milieu   merchandise
melevolent   malevolent   merchant
melibdenen   molybdenum   mercurochrome
mellifluent   mercury
mellow   mercy
melodrama

mere (pool, see mire)		meteor	
meretricious		meteorite	
merganser duck		meteorology	
merge		meter	
meridian		methadone	
meringue		methane	
merited		method	
meritorious		methodology	
mermaid		methyl	
merose	morose	methylene	
mershum	meerschaum	meticulous	
mesa		metier/métier	
mescal		metric	
mescaline		metrical	
mesdames		metronome	
meskeg	muskeg	metropolis	
meskellung	muskellunge	metropolitan	
mesmerize		mettle (courage, see medal, metal)	
mesquite			
message		mews (stables, see muse)	
messenger			
mestizo		mezmorize	mesmerize
mesure	monsieur	mezzanine	
metabolism		mezzo-soprano	
metabolic		miasma	
metal (iron, see medal, mettle)		mica	
metallurgy		microanalysis	
metamorphic		microbe	
metamorphosis		microcosm	
metaphor		microcosmic	
metaphysical		micrometer	
metatarsal		microorganism	
mete (measure, see meat, meet)		micron	
		microscope	
		midevil	medieval

midget
midriff
midst
mien (bearing,
  see mean)
miestro   maestro
miget   midget
might (power,
  see mite)
mignonette
migraine
migrate
migration
migratory
mikado
milapede   millipede
mildew
mileage
milieu
militancy
militant
militarist
military
militia
millenary
  (1,000th anni-
  versary, see
  millinery)
milktoast   milquetoast
millennium
millet
millimeter
milliner
millinery (hats,
  see millenary)
million

millipede
millwright
milquetoast
mime
mimeograph
mimic
mimosa
minaret
minature   miniature
minastrone   minestrone
miner (mine-
  worker, see
  minor)
mineral
mineralogy
minescule   minuscule
minester   minister
minesteral   ministerial
minestration   ministration
minestrone
mingle
miniature
minimum
minion
minister
minks (pl. animal,
  see minx)
minnow
minor (underage,
  see miner)
minority
minow   minnow
minstrel
mintage
minuet
minus

minuscule		misjudgment	
minute (time or small)		misletoe	mistletoe
		mismanage	
minyon	minion	misnomer	
minyonette	mignonette	misogyny	
minx (pert girl, see minks)		misque	miscue
		missal (book, see missile)	
mio	maillot		
miopia	myopia	misshapen	
miopic	myopic	missile (weapon, see missal)	
miracle			
miraculous		mission	
mirage		missionary	
mire (marsh, see mere)		missive	
		misspell	
meeriad	myriad	misstate	
mirr	myrrh	misstep	
mirror		mistake	
mirth		mistletoe	
mirtle	myrtle	mistoso	maestoso
misalliance		mistress	
misanthrope		misure	monsieur
miscalculation		mite (insect, see might)	
miscarriage			
miscegenation		mitigate	
miscellaneous		mitt	
mischief		mitten	
mischievous		mnemonics	
misconception		moan (complain, see mown)	
misconstrue			
miscue		moat (trench, see mote)	
misdemeanor			
miser		mobile	
miserable		moccasin	
misfeasance		modal (logic, see model)	
misinterpretation			

modecum	modicum	momento	memento
model (image, see modal)		momentous	
moderate		monacle	monocle
modernization		monaker	moniker
modes operandi	modus operandi	monarch	
		monastery	
modest		monastic	
modeste	modiste	monator	monitor
modicum		monetary	
modify		monetone	monotone
modish		monger	
modist	modest	Mongoloid	
modiste		mongoose	
modlin	maudlin	mongrel	
modulate		moniker	
modulation		monitor	
modus operandi		monochromatic	
mogul		monocle	
mohair		monogamy	
moist		monogram	
molar		monograph	
molasses		monogyny	
Molatov cocktail	Molotov cocktail	monolithic	
molecular		monologue	
molecule		monomania	
molest		monopoly	
mollify		monostery	monastery
mollusk		monosyllable	
mollycoddle		monotheism	
Molotov cocktail		monotone	
molten		monotonous	
molybdenum		monoxide	
momentary		monsieur	
		monsignor	
		monsoon	
		monster	

monstrosity		morrow	
montage		morsel	
monument		moseleum	mausoleum
moñana	mañana	mortal	
moomoo	muumuu	mortar	
moorage		mortgage	
moose (animal, see mousse)		mortician	
		mortify	
mope		mortise	
moppet		mortuary	
moral (ethics)		mosaic	
morale (spirit)		Moselle wine	
morane	moraine	mosey	
morass		mosque	
moratorium		mosquito	
moray eel		moss	
morays	mores	mote (speak, see moat)	
morbid			
morcel	morsel	motet	
mordant (caustic)		motif	
		motile	
mordent (music)		motion	
		motive	
mores		motley	
morfine	morphine	mottled	
morgage	mortgage	motto	
morgue		mountain	
moribund		mourning (grieving, see morning)	
morning (dawn, see mourning)			
moron		mouse (rodent)	
morose		mousse (dessert, see moose)	
morphine			
morphology		mouton coat	
morray eel	moray eel	mov	mauve

mower
mown (cut down,
  see moan)
moze   mosey
Mozell wine   Moselle wine
mucilage
mucous membrane
mufti
mugger
muggy
mukluk
mulatto
mulberry
mulch
mulct
mullet
multen   molten
multifarious
multifold
Multigraph
multilateral
multilinear
Multilith
multipartite
multiple
multiple sclerosis
multiplicand
multiplicity
multitude
mumble
mummify
mummy
mumu   muumuu
mundane
municipal
munificent

munitions
mural
murcury   mercury
murky
murmur
murr   myrrh
muscatel
muscle (body
  tissue, see
  mussel)
muscular dys-
  trophy
muse (meditate,
  see mews)
museum
mushroom
musician
musilage   mucilage
muskellunge
musket
musketeer
muskrat
muslin
mussel (shellfish,
  see muscle)
mustache
mustard (on
  hot dogs)
mustered (assem-
  bled)
mutable
mutilate
mutineer
mutiny
mutter
mutton

MUTUAL   MYTHOLOGY

mutual   mystic
muumuu   mystify
muzzle   mystique
myopic   myth
myriad   mythical
myrrh   mythological
myrtle   mythology
mysterious

N

nack	knack	natal	
nacreous		natatorium	
nadir		national	
nagging		native	
naive/naïve		nativity	
naivete/naïveté		nattatorium	natatorium
namby-pamby		natty	
napalm		natural	
naphtha		nature	
napom	napalm	naughty	
napsack	knapsack	nausea	
narate	narrate	nauseate	
narcissus		nauseous	
narcissistic		nautical	
narl	gnarl	nautilus	
narcosis		nauty	naughty
narcotic		naval (navy, see	
narrate		navel)	
narrator		nave (church,	
narrow		see knave)	
nasal		navel (belly-	
nascent		button, see	
nash	gnash	naval)	
nasturtium		navigate	
nat	gnat	navigator	

naw	gnaw	nemesis	
nay (no,		nemonics	mnemonics
see neigh)		neolithic	
nazel	nasal	neomycin	
nebulous		neon	
necessary		neophyte	
necessity		nepetism	nepotism
neckerchief		neoplasm	
necklace		nephew	
necktie		nephritis	
necromancy		nepotism	
necrophilia		nerture	nurture
nectar		nervana	nirvana
nectarine		nerve	
need (require,		nervous	
see knead)		nestle	
needle		netting	
ne'er-do-well		nettle	
nefarious		neuclear	nuclear
nefritis	nephritis	neuclei	nuclei
negate		neucleon	nucleon
negative		neucleus	nucleus
neglect		neumatic	pneumatic
negligee		neumonia	pneumonia
negligent		neural	
negligible		neuralgia	
negotiate		neuritis	
negotiation		neurology	
negotiator		neurosis	
Negro		neurotic	
Negroes		neuter	
neice	niece	neutral	
neigh (horse,		neutron	
see nay)		new (recent, see	
neighbor		gnu, knew)	
neither		newel	

nexus		nipple	
niacin		nippy	
nicatine	nicotine	nirvana	
nicety		nisei	
niche		nisi	
nickel		nitch	niche
nickelodeon		nitrate	
nickers	knickers	nitric acid	
nicknack/knick- knack		nitrify	
		nitrite	
nickname		nitrogen	
nicotine		nitroglycerin	
nictitropism	nyctitropism	nob	knob
niece		noble	
niether	neither	nobility	
nieve	naive/naïve	noblesse oblige	
nievete	naivete/ naïveté	nockwurst	knockwurst
		nocturnal	
nifarious	nefarious	nocturne	
niggardly		nocuous (injuri-	
night (evening,		ous, see noxious)	
see knight)		node	
nightingale		nodule	
nihilism		noel/noël	
nimbes	nimbus	noggin	
nimble		noise	
nimbus		noll	knoll
nimonics	mnemonics	nomad	
nimph	nymph	nom de plume	
nimphomaniac	nympho- maniac	nome	gnome
		nomenclature	
nine		nominal	
nineteen		nominate	
ninety		nominclature	nomenclature
ninth		nominee	
niponese	nipponese	nonabsorbent	

nonacceptance
nonaggressive
nonalcoholic
nonbeliever
nonbelligerent
nonblooming
noncense   nonsense
nonchalance
noncoercive
noncombatant
noncombustible
noncommissioned
noncommittal
noncommunist
noncompetitive
noncompliance
nonconductor
nonconformist
noncontroversial
noncorrosive
nondescript
none (nothing,
  see nun)
nonelective
nonentity
nonessential
nonexistence
nonfiction
nonintervention
nonirritant
nonmetallic
nonobjective
nonobsorbent   nonabsorbent
nonpareil
nonpartisan
nonpoisonous

nonproductive
nonprofit
nonrenewable
nonreoccuring   nonrecurring
nonresident
nonrestrictive
nonsectarian
nonsense
non sequitur
nontaxable
nontoxic
nonvascular
nonviolence
noodle
no one
noose
normal
normalcy
nosea   nausea
noseate   nauseate
nostalgia
nostril
nostrum
not (negative,
  see knot)
notable
notarize
notary
notation
notch
noteriety   notoriety
noteworthy
notible   notable
notical   nautical
notice
noticeable

noticing		numb	
notify		number	
notilus	nautilus	numbskull	numskull
notion		numerable	
notoriety		numeral	
notorious		numerous	
no-trump		numismatics	
nougat		numskull	
nought		nun (clergy,	
nourish		see none)	
novacain	novocaine	nuptial	
novel		nural	neural
novelette		nuralgia	neuralgia
novelist		nurish	nourish
novena		nuritis	neuritis
novice		nurology	neurology
novitiate		nurosis	neurosis
novocaine		nurotic	neurotic
noxious (causing		nurvana	nirvana
harm, see		nurse	
nocuous)		nursery	
nozzle		nurture	
nth degree		nusance	nuisance
nuance		nuter	neuter
nubile		nutmeg	
nuckle	knuckle	nutral	neutral
nuclear		nutrient	
nuclei		nutrition	
nucleus		nutritious	
nudity		nutron	neutron
nugat	nougat	nuzzle	
nugget		nylon	
nuisance		nymph	
null		nymphomaniac	
nullify			

O

oafish		oblation
oaken		obligate
oar (paddle, see		obligato	obbligato
or, ore)		obligatory
oasis		oblige
oath		oblique
obalisk	obelisk	obliterate
obasance	obeisance	oblivion
obbligato		oblivious
obcequies	obsequies	oblong
obcequious	obsequious	obloquy
obcidian	obsidian	obnoxious
obdurate		oboe
obedient		oboist
obeisance		obortion	abortion
obelisk		obscene
obese		obscond	abscond
obesity		obscurantism
obey		obscure
obfuscate		obscurity
obituary		obsequies
objection		obsequious
objector		observant
objet d'art		observation
oblate		observatory

observe		occidental	
obsess		occipital	
obsession		occlude	
obsidian		occlusion	
obsolescent		occular	ocular
obsolete		occulist	oculist
obsolve	absolve	occult	
obsorb	absorb	occultism	
obstacle		occupant	
obstain	abstain	occupation	
obstanate	obstinate	occupy	
obstatrician	obstetrician	occur	
obstenancy	obstinacy	occurred	
obstetrical		occurrence	
obstetrician		ocean	
obstetrics		oceanic	
obstinacy		oceanography	
obstinate		ocelot	
obstreperous		ocher	
obstruct		ocident	occident
obstructer		ocidental	occidental
obsurd	absurd	ocipital	occipital
obtain		ociput	occiput
obtrude		o'clock	
obtrusive		oclude	occlude
obtuse		oclusion	occlusion
obverse		octagon	
obviate		octagonal	
obvious		octahedron	
ocarina		octane	
occasion		octave	
occelot	ocelot	octet	
occident (the		octogenarian	
west, see		octopus	
accident)		octoroon	

ocular		ofiolatry	ophiolatry
oculist		often	
ocult	occult	oftener	
ocultism	occultism	ogle	
ocupant	occupant	ogre	
ocupation	occupation	ogreish	
ocur	occur	ohm	
ode		oiliness	
od infinitum	ad infinitum	oily	
odious		ointment	
od nauseam	ad nauseam	okay	
odometer		okra	
odor		old lange zine	auld lang syne
odoriferous		oldster	
odorous		oleaginous	
odulation	adulation	oleander	
od valorem	ad valorem	oleomargarine	
odyssey		oleoresin	
Oedipus		olfactory	
oestrus/estrus		oligarchy	
ofel	offal	Olympic	
ofen	often	om	ohm
offal		omega	
offend		omelet	
offender		omen	
offense		ominous	
offensive		omission	
offertory		omlet	omelet
officer		omnibus	
official		omnipotent	
officialdom		omnipresent	
officiate		omniscient	
officiator		omnivorous	
officious		omph	oomph
offset		onanism	

oncoming		operation	
oncore	encore	operative	
onerous		operator	
ongenue	ingenue/	operetta	
	ingénue	opertune	opportune
onion		ophthalmologist	
onis	onus	opiate	
onix	onyx	opine	
onnomatopoeia	onomato-	opinion	
	poeia	opinionated	
onnus	onus	opium	
onomatopoeia		oponent	opponent
onslaught		oportunism	opportunism
onsomble	ensemble	oportunity	opportunity
ontological		opose	oppose
ontology		oposite	opposite
ontrepreneur	entrepreneur	oposition	opposition
ontourage	entourage	oppertune	opportune
onus		oppertunity	opportunity
onward		oppesite	opposite
onyx		opponent	
oogenesis/		opportune	
oögenesis		opportunistic	
oolong		opportunity	
oomph		oppose	
ooze		opposite	
opacity		opposition	
opal		oppossum	
opalescent		oppress	
opaque		oppression	
opel	opal	opprobrious	
opelescent	opalescent	opprobrium	
opera		oppulence	opulence
operable		opress	oppress
operate		opression	oppression

opt		ordain	
optamism	optimism	ordeal	
opthamologist	ophthalmol- ogist	or d'erve	hors d'oeuvre
		ordinal	
optic		ordinance (law, see	
optical		ordnance)	
optician		ordinarily	
optimism		ordinary	
optimistic		ordinate	
optimum		ordnance	
option		(weapons, see	
optional		ordinance)	
optometrist		ordure	
optometry		ore (metal, see	
opulence		oar, or)	
opus		oregano	
or (conjunction,		oreomycin	aureomycin
see oar, ore)		oreole	oriole
oracle (wise man,		orfice	orifice
see auricle)		organ	
oracular		organdy	
oral (vocal, see		organic	
aural)		organism	
orange		organist	
orangutan		organization	
orate		organize	
orator		organizer	
oratorio		organza	
oratory		orgasm	
orbit		orgiastic	
orbital		orgy	
orcestra	orchestra	oricle	oracle
orchard		orient	
orchestra		oriental	
orchid		orientation	

orifice

origin

original

origination

originator

oriole (bird, see
   aureole)

orison

orlon

ornament

ornamental

ornamentation

ornate

ornathology   ornithology

orneriness

ornery

ornithology

orphan

orphanage

orracle   oracle

orratorio   oratorio

orregano   oregano

or revoir   au revoir

orrifice   orifice

orriole   oriole

orrison   orison

ortopsy   autopsy

orthodontist

orthodoxy

orthogenic

orthopedics

oscillate

oscilloscope

oscine

osculate

osicle   ossicle

osiloscope   oscilloscope

osmosis

osmotic

osprey

ossicle

ossification

ossify

ossillate   oscillate

ossilloscope   oscilloscope

ossine   oscine

ossprey   osprey

ossulate   osculate

ostensible

ostentation

ostentatious

osteopath

ostracism

ostracize

ostrich

ostricism   ostracism

ostricize   ostracize

ostrige   ostrich

otiose

otter

ought (should,
   see aught)

oui (yes, see we)

Ouija board

ounce

ourselves

oust

outboard

outburst

outdistance

outmoded
outpatient
outpouring
outrage
outrageous
outrigger
outsell
outward
outweigh
outwit
ova
ovary
ovation
overalls
overawed
overbearing
overboard
overconfident
overdose
overdraft
overexposure
overhaul
overlap
overruling

overseas
overseer
oversight
overt
overture
overweening
overwhelming
overwrought
overy   ovary
oviparous
ovulate
ovum
owe
owing
owlish
ownership
oxeye daisy
oxidation
oxide
oxidize
oxtail
oxygen
oyster
ozone

P

pabulum
pacemaker
pachyderm
pacific (calm)
Pacific (time or
  ocean)
pacifier
pacify
package
packet
packsack
packsaddle
packyderm   pachyderm
pact
paculiar   peculiar
pacuniary   pecuniary
padding
paddle
paddock
padestrian   pedestrian
padlock
padock   paddock
padre
padrone

paean (song, see
  paeon, peon)
paeon (syllables,
  see paeon,
  peon)
pagan
paganism
pageant
pageantry
pagination
pagoda
pail (bucket, see
  pale)
pain (hurt, see
  pane)
painstaking
paintbrush
painting
pair (two, see
  pare, pear)
pairing (grouping,
  see pareing)
Paisley print
pajama

palace		palor	pallor
paladin		palpable	
paladium	palladium	palpitate	
palamino	palomino	palsy	
palatable		paltry (see	
palatal		poultry)	
palate (mouth,		palygamy	polygamy
see palette,		palzy	palsy
pallet)		pamflet	pamphlet
palatial		pamfleteer	pamphleteer
palaver		pampas	
palbearer	pallbearer	pamper	
pale (white,		pamphlet	
see pail)		pamphleteer	
palea		panacea	
paleate	palliate	panaroma	panorama
paleolithic		panatella	
paleontology		panchromatic	
paletal	palatal	pancreas	
palette (art		panda	
board, see pal-		pandemic	
ate, pallet)		pandemonium	
palfrey		pander	
palid	pallid	pandowdy	
palisade		pane (glass, see	
palitable	palatable	pain)	
palladium		panegyric	
pallbearer		panel	
pallet (bed, see		paneply	panoply
palate, palette)		panhandle	
palliate		panic	
pallid		panicky	
pallor		pannacea	panacea
palmistry		pannel	panel
palomino		panoply	

panorama		paradox	
pansy		parafenalia	parapher-
pantaloon			nalia
pantemine	pantomime	paraffin	
pantheism		parafrase	paraphrase
pantheon		paragon	
panther		paragoric	paregoric
panties		paragraph	
panting		parakeet	
pantomime		parallax	
pantry		parallel	
panty		parallelogram	
pantywaist		paralysis	
Panzer division		paralytic	
panwah	peignoir	paralyze	
papacy		paramecium	
papal		parameter	
papaw		paramount	
papaya		paramour	
papecy	papacy	paramutuel	parimutuel
papier-mache/		paranoia	
papier-maché		parapalegic	paraplegic
papilla		parapet	
papirus	papyrus	paraphernalia	
papoose		paraphrase	
paprika		paraphrastic	
papyrus		paraplegic	
parable		parapsychology	
parabola		parashute	parachute
parachute		parasite	
paracite	parasite	parasol	
paraclete		parasympathetic	
parade		paratrooper	
paradigm		parboil	
paradise		parcel	

parcheesi		parler	parlor
parchment		parley (confer-	
pardon		ence, see	
pardonable		parlay)	
pare (peal, see		parliament	
pair, pear)		parliamentarian	
parecide	parricide	parliamentary	
paregoric		parlor	
parent		Parmesan cheese	
parentage		parmigeon	ptarmigan
parenthesis		parochial	
parenthetic		parody (imita-	
paresis		tion, see parity)	
par excellence		parol (oral)	
parfay	parfait	parole (release)	
parfait		paroxysm	
pariah		parquet	
paridy	parity	parricide	
	(equality)/	parrot	
	parody	parry	
	(imitation)	parsel	parcel
parietal		parshal	partial
parimutuel		parsimony	
paring (cutting,		parsing	
see pairing)		parsley	
parish		parsnip	
parishioner		parson	
paristalsis	peristalsis	parsonage	
paritonitis	peritonitis	parterre	
parity (equality,		partesan	partisan
see parody)		parthenogenesis	
parka		partial	
parlance		participate	
parlay (bet, see			
parley)			

participial		pastor	
participle		pastorate	
particle		pastoral (rural	
particular		life)	
partisan		pastorale (music)	
partisipate	participate	pastrami	
partition		pastry	
partner		pasturage	
partridge		pasture	
parusal	perusal	pasturize	pasteurize
parvenu		pasty	
pary	parry	patchwork	
paschal		pate de foie gras/	
pasha		pâté de foie	
pasify	pacify	gras	
Pasley print	Paisley print	patella	
paso	peso	paten (plate, see	
pasqueflower		patten)	
passable		patent (protec-	
passage		tion)	
passe/passé		paterfamilias	
passerby/passer-by		patern	pattern
passion		paternal	
passionate		paternity	
passive		paternoster	
passtime	pastime	pathetic	
pastachio	pistachio	pathology	
paste		pathos	
pastel		patience (toler-	
pasteurize		ance)	
pastiche		patients (clients)	
pastime		patina	
pasting		patio	

patisserie		peak (top, see	
patois		peek, pique)	
patren	patron	peal (ring, see	
patreot	patriot	peel)	
patriarch		peanut	
patriarchal		pear (fruit, see	
patrician		pare, pair)	
patrimony		pearl (gem, see	
patriot		purl)	
patrol		peasant	
patron		pebble	
patronage		pecable	peccable
patronize		pecant	peccant
patronymic		pecan	
patroon		peccable	
patten (shoe, see		peccadillo	
paten)		peccant	
patter		peccary	
pattern		pecon	pecan
patty shell		pectin	
patuitary	pituitary	pectoral	
patunia	petunia	peculiar	
paucity		pecuniary	
paunchy		pedacure	pedicure
pauper		pedagree	pedigree
pause		pedagogue	
pavement		pedagogy	
pavilion		pedal (lever, see	
paving		peddle)	
pawnbroker		pedament	pediment
payola		pedantic	
peace (calm, see		peddle (sell, see	
piece)		pedal)	
peach		pedegogue	pedagogue
peacock		pedegogy	pedagogy
pea jacket		pedentic	pedantic

pedestal		penance	
pedestrian		penant	pennant
pediatrician		penate	pennate
pediatrics		pence	
pediatrist	podiatrist	penchant	
pedicure		pencil	
pedigree		pendant (orna-	
pediment		ment)	
pedistal	pedestal	pendent (hanging	
pedology		down)	
pee jacket	pea jacket	pendulum	
peek (peep, see		penecillin	penicillin
peak, pique)		penetent	penitent
peel (strip, see		penetential	penitential
peal)		penetrate	
peenockle	pinochle	penetrable	
peer (an equal,		penguin	
see pier)		penicillin	
peerless		peninsula	
peeve		penitent	
peewee		penitential	
peignoir		penitrate	penetrate
pejorative		penmanship	
Pekingese		pennance	penance
pekoe		pennant	
pelagic		pennate	
pelaver	palaver	pennicillia	penicillin
pelican		penniless	
pellet		penninsula	peninsula
pell-mell		penochle	pinochle
pelvic		penology	
pelvis		penorious	penurious
pemento	pimento	pension	
pemmican		pentagon	
penal		pentahedron	
penalty		pentameter	

pentateuch		perceptible	
pentathlon		perch	
Pentecostal		perchance	
pentegon	pentagon	perchase	purchase
penthouse		percieve	perceive
penuche		percipient	
penuchle/		percipitate	precipitate
pinochle		percolate	
penultimate		percussion	
penurious		perdicament	predicament
penury		perdition	
penwah	peignoir	perdurable	
peon (worker, see		peregrinate	
paean, paeon)		peremptory	
peonage		pereneum	perineum
peony		perennial	
pepilla	papilla	perentheses	parentheses
pepper		perenthesis	parenthesis
pepsin		perenthetic	parenthetic
peptone		perfect	
pequant	piquant	perfectible	
peracycle	pericycle	perfecto	
peralysis	paralysis	perfer	prefer
peralytic	paralytic	perfidy	
perambulate		perforate	
peramecium	paramecium	perforce	
perameter	parameter	perform	
peranha	piranha	perfume	
per annum		perfunctory	
perapatetic	peripatetic	pergure	perjure
percale		perhaps	
per capita		periah	pariah
perceive		pericycle	
percent		periferal	peripheral
percentage		perifery	periphery
percept		perigee	

perihelion		perpetual	
peril		perpetuate	
perilous		perpetuity	
perimeter		perpindicular	perpendicular
perineum		perplex	
period		perport	purport
periodical		perscription	prescription
peripatetic		persecute	
peripheral		persecutor	
periphery		perservative	preservative
periscope		perserve	preserve
perish		perseverance	
perishable		persevere	
peristalsis		persiflage	
peritonitis		persimmon	
periwinkle		persipient	percipient
perjure		persist	
perjury		persistence	
perky		personable	
permanent		personage	
permeable		personal (per-	
permeate		son, see person-	
permissible		nel)	
permission		persona non grata	
permissive		personify	
permit		personnel (em-	
permutation		ployes, see per-	
pernicious		sonal)	
perochial	parochial	perspective	
perogative	prerogative	perspectus	prospectus
perorate		perspicacious	
perouette	pirouette	perspicacity	
peroxide		perspicuity	
perpatuity	perpetuity	perspire	
perpendicular		persuade	
perpetrate		persuant	pursuant

persuasion		pettiness	
persue	pursue	petty	
persuit	pursuit	petuitary	pituitary
pertain		petulance	
pertinacious		petulant	
pertinent		petunia	
perturb		Peugeot	
perturbable		pewter	
pertussis		pfennig	
peruke		phalanx	
perusal		phallic	
pervade		phallus	
perverbial	proverbial	phantom	
perverse		pharmaceutical	
pervert		pharmacology	
perywinkle	periwinkle	pharmacy	
pesel	pestle	pharynx	
peso		phase (facet, see faze)	
pessimism		
pesticide		pheasant	
pestiferous		phenobarbital	
pestilent		phenomenon	
pestle		phenomenal	
petal		phenotype	
petard		philanderer	
petcock		philanthropy	
petella	patella	philately	
petite		philharmonic	
petition		Philipino	Filipino
petit jury		philippic	
petits fours		philodendron	
petits pois		philology	
petrify		philosophy	
petroleum		philter (potion, see filter)	
petrology		
petticoat		phlegm	

phlegmatic	physician
phlogistic	physics
phobia	physiognomy
phobic	physiology
phoebe	physiotherapy
phonetic	physique
phonics	pianist
phonograph	piano
phosphate	piasano
phosphorescence	piazza
phosphorus	pibold piebald
photo	pica
photoelectric	picaresque
photoengraving	picayune
photogenic	piccalilli
photograph	piccolo
photography	pickerel
photogravure	picket
photomural	pickle
photon	pickyune picayune
photosensitive	picnic
photosphere	picnicking
photostat	pictograph
photosynthesis	pictorial
phototaxis	picture
phototropic	picturesque
phrase	picuniary pecuniary
phraseology	piddling
phrenetic/frenetic	pidgin English
phrenology	(language, see
phylogeny	pigeon)
phylum	piebald
physic	piece (segment,
physical (about	see peace)
bodies, see	piece de resistance/
fiscal)	pièce de résis-
	tance

piedmont

pier (dock, see
  peer)

pierce

piety

pigeon (bird, see
  pidgin)

pigment

pigmy   pygmy

pigsty

pilage   pillage

pilaster

pilchard

pilfer

pilgrim

pilgrimage

piling

pillage

pillar

pillory

pillow

pilon   pylon

pilorus   pylorus

pilot

pimento

pimpernel

pimple

pinacle   pinnacle

pinafore

pinate   pinnate

pince-nez

pincers

pineal gland

pineapple

pininsula   peninsula

pinnace

pinnacle

pinnate

pinochle/penuchle

pinsers   pincers

pinultimate   penultimate

pioneer

piorrhea   pyorrhea

pious

pipe

pipette

piping

piquant

pique (provoke
  or score, see
  peak, peek)

piranha

piracy

pirate

pirex   pyrex

pirosis   pyrosis

pirouette

piscatorial

pistachio

pistil (flower
  part)

pistol (gun)

piston

pitapat

pitch

pitcher

piteable   pitiable

piteous

pithy

pitiable

pitiful		plait (briad, see	
pitiless		plate)	
piton		plaiting (to braid,	
pittance		see plating)	
pittapat	pitapat	plane (geometry,	
pituitary		see plain)	
pity		planet	
pivot		planetary	
pixy		planograph	
pizza		plantain	
pizzeria		plantation	
plabian	plebian	plaque (plate,	
placable		see plack)	
placard		plasebo	placebo
placate		plasid	placid
placebo		plasma	
placement		plaster	
placenta		plastic	
placible	placable	plasticity	
placid		platapus	platypus
plack (coin, see		plate (dish, see	
plaque)		plait)	
placket		plateau	
plagerist	plagiarist	platen	
plagiarism		plater	platter
plagiarist		platetude	platitude
plagiary		platform	
plague		plating (to coat,	
plaid		see plaiting)	
plain (flat, see		platinum	
plane)		platitude	
plaint		platoon	
plaintiff (suer)		platten	platen
plaintive (mourn-		platter	
ful)		platypus	

plaudit		plumber	
plausible		plume	
plaza		plumer	plumber
plazma	plasma	plummet	
plea		plunder	
plead		plunge	
pleasant		pluperfect	
please		plural	
pleasure		plurality	
pleat		plurisy	pleurisy
plebian		plutocracy	
plebiscite		plutonium	
plecenta	placenta	plyers	pliers
pledge		pneumatic	
plenary		pneumonia	
plenipotentiary		poacher	
plenteous		pocket	
plesant	pleasant	podiatrist	
plete	pleat	podium	
pleurisy		poem (verse,	
plexus		see pome)	
pliable		poet	
pliant		poetic	
pliers		poet laureate	
plight		pogrom	
plinth		poh	
plistocene	pleistocene	poi	
plodit	plaudit	poignancy	
plotter		poignant	
plowshare		poinsettia	
plucky		pointillism	
plum (fruit, see		poison	
plumb)		poker	
plumage		polar	
plumb (weight,		polarization	
see plum)		Polaroid	

pole (stick, see poll)		polonaise	
polemic		poltice	poultice
poler	polar	poltroon	
polerization	polarization	poltry	poultry
Poleroid	Polaroid	polyandry	
polestar		polychromatic	
polety	polity	polyclinic/poli-clinic	
pole vault		polyethylene	
polex	pollex	polygamy	
policeman		polyglot	
policlinic/poly-clinic		polygon	
policy		polygyny	
poliglot	polyglot	polyhedron	
polinate	pollinate	polyp	
polio		polyphonic	
poliomyelitis		polytechnic	
polip	polyp	pomade	
polish		pome (fruit, see poem)	
polite		pomegranate	
political		pommel (saddle, see pummel)	
politico		pompadour	
politics		pompano	
polity		pompon	
polka		pompous	
poll (voting place, see pole)		pomposity	
pollen		poncho	
pollex		ponder	
pollinate		pongee	
polliwog		pon-ne	pince-nez
pollute		pontiff	
pollution		pontifical	
Pollyanna		pontoon	
pollywog	polliwog	pony	

poo	pooh
poodle	
poor (needy, see pore, pour)	
poper	pauper
popery	
poplar (tree, see popular)	
poplin	
popourri	potpourri
poppy	
populace (masses, see populous)	
popular (approved, see poplar)	
populate	
Populist	
populous (thickly settled, see populace)	
porcelain	
porcupine	
pore (small opening, see poor, pour)	
poriferous	
porige	porridge
pornographic	
pornography	
porous	
porosity	
porpoise	
porpus	porpoise
porridge	
Porsche	

porselain	porcelain
portable (move-able, see potable)	
portage (carry overland, see pottage)	
portal	
porteco	portico
portege	portage
portend	
portent	
portfolio	
portico	
portion	
portly	
portrait	
portray	
porus	porous
posess	possess
poshion	potion
posit	
position	
positive	
posse	
possess	
possible	
possum	oppossum
postage	
postal	
poster	
posterior	
posterity	
posthaste	
posthumous	
postimpressionism	

postmortem
postnatal
postorbital
postponable
postponement
postscript
postulate
postumous   posthumous
posture
posy (flower,
   see posse)
potable (drink-
   able, see port-
   able)
potage   pottage
potash
potassium
potation
potato
potency
potent
potentate
potential
potery   pottery
potion
potlatch
potpourri
pottage (soup,
   see portage)
pottery
poultice
poultry
pounce
pound
pour (flow,
   see pore, poor)

pousse-café
poverty
powder
power
powwow
pox
pozit   posit
pozy   posy
practicable
practical
practice
practitioner
pragmatic
prairie
praise (admire,
   see prase)
praline
prance
prankish
prarie   prairie
prase (stone, see
   praise)
prasentable   presentable
prasume   presume
prate
prattle
prawn
pray (plead, see
   prey)
prayer
preach
preacher
preamble
precancel
precarious
precaution

precede
precedent (first,
   see president)
precept
precinct
precind   prescind
precious
precipice
precipitant
precipitate
precis/précis
   (summary)
precise (exact)
precision
preclude
preclusion
precocious
preconception
precondition
precursor
predator
predecessor
predelection   predilection
predestination
predetermine
predetor   predator
predicament
predicate
predict
predictable
predilection
predispose
predominant
pre-eminent/-
   preeminent
pre-empt

preen
pre-existence
prefabricate
preface
prefect
prefer
preferable
preferred
preform   perform
pregnancy
pregnant
prehensile
prehistoric
preiminent   pre-eminent/-
                           preeminent
prejudice
prelate
preliminary
prelude
premature
premedical
premeditate
premenition   premonition
premier (official,
   see premiere,
   primer)
premiere (first
   showing, see
   premier, primer)
premise
premium
premolar
premonition
premonitory
prenatal
preoccupy

preordain
prepare
preponderance
preportion   proportion
prepose   propose
preposition
prepossessing
preposterous
prerequisite
prerogative
presage
Presbyterian
presbytery
prescience
prescind
prescribe
prescription
presdadigitation   prestidigita-
                    tion
present
presentable
presentiment
presentment
preservation
preservative
preserve
preside
president (chief,
  see precedent)
presidio
presidium
presinct   precinct
presind   prescind
presious   precious
presipice   precipice
pressure

prestidigitation
prestige
presto
presume
presumption
presumptuous
presuppose
presure   pressure
pretend
pretender
pretense
pretentious
preternatural
pretext
prettify
pretty
pretzel
prevail
prevalent
prevaricate
prevent
preverbial   proverbial
preview
previous
previso   proviso
prevoke   provoke
prey (victom, see
  pray)
pricipitant   precipitant
pricipitate   precipitate
prickle
prideful
priest
prig
priggish
primacy

prima donna		prize	
prima facie		probable	
primal		probate	
primarily		probation	
primary		probe	
primate		probiscis	proboscis
primer (first text, see premier, premiere)		probity	
		problem	
		proboscis	
primeval		procedural	
primitive		procedure	
primogeniture		proceed	
primordial		procenium	proscenium
primrose		process	
principal (main teacher; see principle)		procession	
		proclaim	
		proclivity	
principally		proconsul	
principle (general truth, see principal)		procrastinate	
		procreate	
		proctor	
principled		procure	
printable		prodegy	prodigy
prior		prodigal	
prioress		prodigious	
priority		prodigy	
prisidium	presidium	produce	
prism		product	
prison		profalactic	prophylactic (device)
pristine			
prittify	prettify	profilaxis	prophylaxis (the prevention of disease)
privacy			
private			
privilege		profane	
privy council		profanity	

profecy	prophecy (noun), prophesy (verb)	prohibit	
		prohibition	
		project	
		projectile	
profer	proffer	projector	
profess		prolactin	
profession		proletariat	
professor		proliferate	
profetic	prophetic	prolific	
proffer .		prolix	
proficiency		prologue	
proficient		promenade	
profilactic	prophylactic (device)	promentory	promontory
		prominence	
profilaxis	prophylaxis (the prevention of disease)	promiscuity	
		promiscuous	
		promise	
		promissory	
profile		promolgate	promulgate
profit (gain, see prophet)		promontory	
		promote	
profitable		prompt	
profligate		promulgate	
profound		promulgator	
profundity		pron	prawn
profuse		prone	
profusion		pronoun	
progenitor		pronounce	
progeny		pronunciation	
prognosis		propaganda	
program		propagate	
programing/pro-gramming		propagation	
		propane	
progress		propeganda	propaganda
progressive		propel	

propellant
propeller
propensity
proper
property
prophalactic   prophylactic
                    (device)
prophalaxis   prophylaxis
                    (the preven-
                    tion of
                    disease)
prophecy (noun,
  see prophesy)
phophesier
prophesy (verb,
  see prophecy)
prophet (pre-
  dictor, see profit)
prophetic
prophylactic (de-
  vice)
prophylaxis (the
  prevention of
  disease)
propinquity
propitiate
propitious
proponent
proportion
propose
proposition
propound
proprietor
propriety
propulsion

prorate
prosaic
prosaically
proscenium
proscribe
prosecute
proselyte
prosenium   proscenium
prosody
prospect
prospectus
prosper
prosperity
prosperous
prostate (gland,
  see prostrate)
prostitute
prostrate (prone,
  see prostate)
prosy
protagonist
protazoan   protozoan
protean (change-
  able, see pro-
  tein)
protecol   protocol
protect
protectorate
protege/protégé
protein (chemical,
  see protean)
pro tempore
protest
Protestant
protocol

proton		pseudonym	
protoplasm		psoriasis	
prototype		psychedelic	
protozoan		psychiatry	
protrude		psychic	
protrusion		psychoanalysis	
protuberance		psychoanalyze	
provecation	provocation	psychodelic	psychedelic
provender		psychodrama	
proverb		psychological	
proverbial		psychology	
provide		psychometry	
providence		psychopathic	
providential		psychosis (illness,	
province		see sycosis)	
provincial		psychosomatic	
provision		psychosurgery	
proviso		psychotherapeutics	
provocation		psychotherapy	
provocative		ptarmigan	
provoke		pterodactyl	
provost marshal		ptomaine	
prowess		puberty	
prowler		pubic	
proximity		public	
proxy		publication	
prozaic	prosaic	publicist	
prozy	prosy	publicity	
prude		publicize	
prudent		publish	
prurient		pucker	
prussic acid		pudding	
psalm		puddle	
psalmody		pudgy	
pseudo		pueblo	

puerile

puerility

puffy

Pugeot   Peugeot

pugilist

pugnacious

puissance

pulchritude

pulchritudinous

pullet

pulley

pulmonary

pulpit

pulque

pulsate

pulverize

puma

pumice

pummel (beat,
    see pommel)

pumpernickel

pumpkin

punative   punitive

punctilious

punctual

punctuate

puncture

pundit

pungent

punish

punitive

punster

pupa

pupil

puppet

puppy

purchase

purfidy   perfidy

puree/purée

purgatory

purge

purifier

Puritan

puritanical

purl (to knit,
    see pearl)

purlieu

purloin

purple

purport

purpose

purr

purse

purser

purslane

pursuant

pursue

pursuit

purvey

purview

pusillanimous

puter   pewter

pustule

put (place, see
    putt)

putrefy

putrescent

putrid

putt (golf stroke,
    see put)

puttee (leg cloth)
putty (for fixing
   windows)
puzzle
pygmy
pylon
pylorus
pyorrhea
pyramid

pyre
Pyrex
pyrites
pyromaniac
pyrosis
pyrotechnics
Pyrrhic victory
python

Q

quackery

quadragenarian

quadrangle

quadrant

quadrilateral

quadroon

quadruped

quadruple

quaff

quagmire

quail

quaint

qualify

qualitative

quality

qualm

quandary

quantify

quantity

quantum

quarantine

quarrel

quarry (excava-
tion, see query)

quarter

quartet

quarto

quartz

quasar

quasijudicial/
quasi-judicial

quatrain

quaver

quay (wharf, see
key)

quazar   quasar

quean (wench,
see queen)

queasy

queen (woman
ruler, see quean)

queer

quell

quench

querulous

query (question,
see quarry)

quest

question

questionnaire

quetzal
queue (line, see
  cue)
quibble
quiddity
quid pro quo
quien sabe
quiescent
quiet (silent, see
  quit, quite)
quietus
quince
quinine
quintessence
quintet
quintuple
quipped
quipster
quire (25 sheets,
  see choir)

quirk
quisine   cuisine
quisling
quit (end, see
    quiet, quite)
quite (total, see
    quiet, quit)
quiver
quixotic
quizling   quisling
quizzed
quizzical
quoin (building
   angle, see
   coign, coin)
quonset
quorum
quota
quotient

R

rabbet (groove,
  see rabbit,
  rarebit)
rabbi
rabbinical
rabbit (animal,
  see rabbet,
  rarebit)
rabble
rabid
rabies
raccoon
racconteur   raconteur
rachet   ratchet
racial
racist
racket
racketeer
racoon   raccoon
raconteur
racy
rader   raider
radeum   radium
radeus   radius
radei   radii

radial
radiant
radiate
radiator
radical
radii
radioactive
radiology
radiosensitive
radiosonde
radiotherapy
radish
radium
radius
raffia
raffish
raffle
ragamuffin
ragatta   regatta
ragged
raglan
ragweed
raider
raillery
railroad

raiment		rapport	
rain (water, see		rapscallion	
reign, rein)		rapsody	rhapsody
raindeer	reindeer	rapt (intent, see	
raise (elevate,		rapped,	
see raze)		wrapped)	
raisin		rapture	
raith	wraith	rapturous	
raja		raquiem	requiem
rakish		rarebit (cheese	
ralere	raillery	dish, see rabbet,	
rally		rabbit)	
rambler		rarefy	
ramekin		rarely	
rament	raiment	rarity	
ramification		rasberry	raspberry
rampage		rascal	
rampant		rasher	
rampart		rasin	raisin
ramshackle		raspberry	
rancid		rasping	
rancor		ratchet	
rancorous		rathskeller	
random		ratify	
rankle		ratifier	
ransack		ratio	
ransid	rancid	ratiocination	
ransom		rational (reason-	
rant (rave, see		able)	
rent)		rationale (basis)	
rapacious		rationalize	
rapid		ratskeller	rathskeller
rapier		rattan	
rapine		rattle	
rapped (hit, see		raucous	
rapt, wrapped)		ravage	

ravel		reaper	
ravenous		reappearance	
ravine		reappoint	
ravioli		rearmament	
ravish		rearrange	
raw		reason	
rayon		reassemble	
raze (demolish,		reassign	
see raise)		reassure	
razor		reath	wreath
razzle-dazzle		reawaken	
reabsorb		rebate	
reactionary		rebellion	
reactor		rebirth	
read (under-		rebuff	
stand, see reed)		rebuke	
readable		rebus	
readily		rebut	
readjustment		rebuttal	
readmission		recalcitrant	
readmit		recallable	
readmittance		recant	
ready		recap	
reaf	reef	recappable	
reaffirm		recapitulate	
reagent (sub-		recede	
stance, see		receipt	
regent)		receive	
real (true, see		recency	
reel)		recent	
realistic		recepe	recipe
reallocation		receptacle	
realm		reception	
realtor		receptor	
realty		recesitate	resuscitate
ream		recession	

recidivism		recoup	
recind	rescind	recourse	
recipe		recovery	
recipient		recreant	
reciprocate		recreation	
reciprocity		recrimination	
recision		recrudescence	
recission	rescission	recruit	
recitation		rectal	
recite		rectangle	
reck	wreck	rectify	
reckon		rectilinear	
reclaim		rectitude	
reclamation		rector	
recliner		rectory	
recluse		rectum	
recognize		recumbent	
recoil		recupe	recoup
recollect		recuperate	
recommend		recur	
recommit		recurrence	
recompense		recycle	
reconasance	reconnais-	redeem	
	sance	redemption	
reconcile		redevelopment	
recondite		rediculous	ridiculous
reconnaissance		redily	readily
reconnoiter		redingote	
reconsider		rediscovery	
reconsign		redolent	
reconsile	reconcile	redouble	
reconstitute		redound	
reconstruction		redress	
reconvene		reduce	
reconvert		redundant	
record		reduplication	

reed (stem, see
  read)
reef
reek (smell, see
  wreak)
reel (spin, see
  real)
reelect
reem   ream
reemergence
reemploy
reenact
reengage
reenlistment
reenter
reestablish
reexamine
referable
referee
reference
referendum
referral
referred
refine
refinery
reflect
reflector
reflex
reforestation
reformation
reformatory
refract
refractory
refrain
refrigerate

refuge
refugee
refund
refurbish
refuse
refusal
refute
regal (splendid)
regale (feed)
regalia
regard
regatta
regemen   regimen
regement   regiment
regeneration
regent (ruler, see
  reagent)
regergitate   regurgitate
regicide
regime
regimen
regiment
region
register
registrant
registrar
registry
regius
regress
regret
regrettable
regular
regulate
regurgitate
rehabilitate

rehearse		relieve	
reign (rule, see		religion	
rain, rein)		relinquish	
reimbursement		relish	
rein (straps, see		relm	realm
rain, reign)		relocation	
reincarnation		reluctant	
reindeer		remady	remedy
reinforcement		remain	
reinsert		remainder	
reinstate		remand	
reintegrate		remarkable	
reintroduce		remarriage	
reinvest		remedial	
reissue		remedy	
reiterate		remember	
reject		remembrance	
rejoice		remenisce	reminisce
rejoinder		reminder	
rejuvenate		reminisce	
rekindle		remiss	
relapse		remit	
relate		remittable	
relative		remittance	
relavant	relevant	remittor	
relax		remnant	
relay		remonstrate	
release		remorse	
relegate		remote	
relent		removable	
relevant		removal	
reliable		remuneration	
reliant		ren	wren
relic		renagade	renegade
relief		renaissance	

rench	wrench	repercussion	
render		repertoire	
rendezvous		repertory	
rendition		repetition	
renegade		rephrase	
renege		replaca	replica
renegotiate		replace	
renewal		replenish	
renig	renege	replete	
rennet		repletion	
renominate		replica	
renovate		reply	
renown		report	
rent (each		reportorial	
month, see		repose	
rant)		repository	
rentgen	roentgen	repossess	
renunciation		reppercussion	repercussion
reoccupy		reprehend	
reorganization		repremand	reprimand
reostat	rheostat	represent	
repair		repress	
reparation		repression	
repartee		repressive	
repast		reprieve	
repatoire	repertoire	reprimand	
repatory	repertory	reprisal	
repayable		reproach	
repeal		reprobate	
repeat		reproduce	
repel		reproduction	
repellent		reproof	
repent		reptile	
repentance		republic	
reper	reaper	repudiate	
reperation	reparation	repugnant	

repulse
repulsive
reputable
reputation
request
requiem
requirement
requisite
requital
requite
resale
resavoir   reservoir
rescind
rescission
rescue
research
resedue   residue
resemble
resent
reseprocity   reciprocity
resergent   resurgent
reserrect   resurrect
reservation
reserve
reservoir
resesitate   resuscitate
reside
residence (home,
  see residents)
resident
residential
residents
  (dwellers, see
  residence)
residual
residivism   recidivism

residue
resign
resilient
resin
resist
resister (one who
  resists)
resistor (elec-
  trical)
resolution
resolve
resonance
resort
resound
resource
respect
respectable
respective
respiration
respiratory
respite
resplendent
response
responsible
responsive
rest (sleep, see
  wrest)
restaurant
restaurateur
restitution
restive
restoration
restrain
restrant   restaurant
restrict
result

resultant		revenge
resume		revenue
resumption		reverberate
resurgent		revere
resurrect		reverent
resuscitate		reverie
retail		reverse
retaliate		reversion
retard		revert
retch (vomit,		review (go over,
see wretch)		see revue)
retention		revile
reticent		revise
retina		revision
retire		revitalize
retna	retina	revival
retoric	rhetoric	revivify
retort		revocable
retract		revoke
retread		revolution
retrial		revolver
retribution		revue (skits, see
retrieve		review)
retroactive		revulsion
retrocession		reward
retrogression		rezilient	resilient
retrospect		rhapsody
retroversion		rheostat
revalle	reveille	rhetoric
reveal		rheumatic
revear	revere	rheumatism
reveille		rheumatoid
revel		rhinestone
revelation		rhinitis
revelry		rhinoceros

rhombus
rhubarb
rhyme (poetry,
  see rime)
rhythm
ribald
ribbing
ribbon
riboflavin
riccochet   ricochet
rickets
rickey
rickrack
ricksha
ricochet
riddance
riddle
ridge
ridicule
ridiculous
riffle (ripple, see
  rifle)
riffraff
rifle (gun/ran-
  sack, see riffle)
rift
rigamarole/rig-
  marole
riga mortis   rigor mortis
rige   ridge
right (true, see
  write, rite,
  wright)
righteous
rigid

rigidity
rigmarole/riga-
  marole
rigor
rigor mortis
rigorous
rime (frost, see
  rhyme)
rinestone   rhinestone
rinitis   rhinitis
rinoceros   rhinoceros
rinse
riot
ripcord
ripen
ripple
rise
riskay   risque
risky
risotto
risque/risqué
rite (ritual, see
  right, wright,
  write)
ritualistic
rival
rivalry
rivulet
roach
roam (wander,
  see Rome)
roan
roar
roast
robbery

robin		root	
rocketry		Roquefort cheese	
rococo		Rorschach test	
rocous	raucous	rosary	
rodent		roseate	
rodeo		Rosetta stone	
roe (doe, see row)		rosette	
		Rosh Hashana	
roentgen		Roshock test	Rorschach test
rogue		rosin	
roil		roster (roll, see rooster)	
roister			
Rokfort cheese	Roquefort cheese	rostrum	
		rotary	
role (function)		rotate	
roll (roster)		rotenone	
rollicking		rotery	rotary
roly-poly/rolypoly		rotisserie	
romaine lettuce		rotogravure	
romance		rotosection	
rombus	rhombus	rotten	
Rome (city, see roam)		rotund	
		rotunda	
romper		roue/roué	
rompus room	rumpus room	roudy	rowdy
rondeau (poem, see rondo)		rouge	
		rough	
rondevous	rendezvous	roulette	
rondo (music, see rondeau)		roundelay	
		rouse	
rookery		rout (expel)	
rookie		route (road)	
roommate		routine	
rooster (chicken, see roster)		row (paddle, see roe)	
		rowdy	

royal		rumage	rummage
rozeate	roseate	rumatic	rheumatic
Rozetta stone	Rosetta stone	rumatism	rheumatism
rozin	rosin	rumatoid	rheumatoid
rua	roue/roué	rumba	
Rubaiyat		rumble	
rubarb	rhubarb	ruminant	
rubber		rummage	
rubbish		rummy	
rubble		rumor	
rubella		rumple	
Rubiat	Rubaiyat	rumpus room	
rubric		runcible spoon	
ruche		rupee	
rucksack		rupture	
ruction		rural	
rudder		ruse	
ruddy		russet	
rude		Russell (name,	
rudiment		see rustle)	
rue		rustic	
ruen	ruin	rustle (sound or	
ruff	rough	steal, see	
ruffian		Russell)	
ruffle		rutabaga	
rugged		rutine	routine
ruin		rythm	rhythm
ruinous		rye (seed, see	
ruler		wry)	
rulette	roulette		

S

sabatage	sabotage	sacroiliac	
Sabbath		sacrosanct	
sabbatical		sacum	succumb
saber		saddle	
sable		sadist	
sabotage		sadistic	
saboteur		safari	
sac (pouch in animal, see sack)		safety	
		saffron	
		safire	sapphire
saccharine		saga	
sacede	secede	sagacious	
sacession	secession	sagebrush	
sachel	satchel	sahib	
sachet		sail (canvas, see sale)	
sack (bag, see sac)		salacious	
		salad	
sackcloth		salamander	
sacral		salami	
sacrament		salary	
sacred		salatary	salutary
sacrifice		sale (selling, see sail)	
sacrilegious			
sacristy			

salecism	solecism	sanatorium	
salenium	selenium	(health resort,	
salient		see sanitarium)	
saline		sanctify	
salinity		sanctimonious	
saliva		sanction	
salivate		sanctuary	
sallow		sandal	
salm	psalm	sandwich	
salmagundi		sane (rational,	
salmon		see seine)	
salon (room)		sang-froid	
saloon (bar)		sanguine	
salstice	solstice	sanitarium	
salubility	solubility	(hospital, see	
salubrious		sanatorium)	
salutary (reme-		sanitary	
dial, see soli-		sanity	
tary)		sanpan	sampan
salutation		Sanskrit	
salute		sans serif	
salvage (save,		sanwich	sandwich
see selvage)		saonce	seance
salvation		sapena	subpoena
salve		sapient	
salvo		sapodilla	
samantics	semantics	sapphire	
sameri	samurai	sapsago	
samon	salmon	sarape/serape	
samovar		sarcasm	
sampan		sarcastic	
sample		sarcophagus	
samurai		sardine	
sanata	sonata	sardonic	
sanatary	sanitary	sargasso	

sargent	sergeant	sav	salve
sari		savage	
sarong		savanna	
sarsaparilla		savant	
sartorial		savior	
sashay	sachet	savoir-faire	
sasheate	satiate	savor	
sasparilla	sarsaparilla	savoy	
sassafras		sawyer	
satallite	satellite	saxophone	
satanic		scabbard	
satchel		scabrous	
sate		scaffold	
sateen		scalawag	
satellite		scald (what boil-	
sater	satyr	ing water does,	
saterist	satirist	see scold)	
saternine	saturnine	scale	
satiate		scalene	
satin		scallion	
satire		scallop	
satirist		scalp	
satisfaction		scalpel	
satisfy		scaly	
satual	satchel	scamper	
saturate		scan	
saturnine		scandalize	
satyr		scanty	
sauce		scapegoat	
sauerkraut		scapula	
sauna		scar	
saunter		scarce	
sausage		scarcity	
saute/sauté		scare	
sauterne		scarf	

scarlet
scathe
scatterbrain
scavenge
scenario
scene
scenery
scent (odor, see
    cent, sent)
scents (pl. odors,
    see cense, cents,
    sense)
scepter
scerge   scourge
scerrilous   scurrilous
scervy   scurvy
schedule
schematic
scheme
scherzo
schism
schizoid
schizophrenia
schmaltz
schnapps
schnauzer
scholar
scholastic
schooner
schottische
schuss
sciatic nerve
science
scimitar
scintillate

scion
scissor
sclerosis
scoff
scold (reprimand,
    see scald)
scooter
scope
scorch
scorn
scorpion
scoundrel
scour
scourge
scowl
scrabble
scramble
scratch
scrawl
scrawny
scream
screech
screen
scribble
scribe
scrimmage
scrimp
script
scripture
scroll
scrotum
scrounge
scruff
scruple
scrupulous

scrutinize
scuba
scuff
scuffle
sculduggery   skulduggery
scull (boat, see
   skull)
scullery
scullion
sculptor
sculptural
scuppernong
scurrilous
scurry
scurvy
scuttle
scuttlebutt
scythe
sea (ocean,
   see see)
seam (sewing, see
   seem)
seaman (sailor,
   see semen)
seamstress
seance
sear (burn, see
   seer)
search
searra   sierra
searsucker   seersucker
season
secede
secession
seclude

secondary
secrecy
secret (mystery,
   see secrete)
secretary
secrete (give off,
   see secret)
secretive
sect
sectarian
section
sector
secular
secure
security
sedament   sediment
sedan
sedate
sedative
sedentary
sedge
sediment
sedition
seduce
sedulous
see (perceive,
   see sea)
seed (grain, see
   cede)
seem (appear, see
   seam)
seemly
seepage
seer (prophet, see
   sear)

seersucker
seesaw
seethe
sege   sedge
segment
segregate
seine (net, see
  sane)
seismograph
seize
seizure
selacious   salacious
seldom
select
selenium
self-confidence
self-conscious
self-discipline
self-evident
self-explanatory
self-expression
self-indulgence
self-preservation
self-reliance
self-respect
self-righteous
self-sacrifice
selfsame
self-satisfied
seller (person,
  see cellar)
selvage (edge,
  see salvage)
semantics
semaphore

semblance
semelina   semolina
semen (sperm,
  see seaman)
semester
semiautomatic
semicircle
semicolon
semifinalist
seminal
seminar
seminary
semiphore   semaphore
semiprecious
Semitic
semmetry   symmetry
semolina
sena   senna
senario   scenario
senate
senator
senile
senior
senna
senor/señor
sensation
sense (intelli-
  gence, see
  cense, cents,
  scents)
senses (sensations,
  see census)
sensitive
sensitize
sensory

sensual
sensuous
sent (dispatched,
  see cent, cense,
  scents)
sentament   sentiment
sentence
sentenal   sentinel
sententious
sentience
sentiment
sentinel
sentry (guard,
  see century)
separate
sepia
septer   scepter
septet
septic
septuagenarian
septum
sepulcher
sepulchral
sequel
sequence
sequential
sequester
sequin
sequoia
seraglio
serape/sarape
seraphim
serch   search
sercumb   succumb
serefim   seraphim

serenade
serendipity
serene
serenity
serf (slave, see
  surf)
serfdom
serge (fabric,
  see surge)
sergeant
serial (sequence,
  see cereal)
series
serif
serious
sermon
serpent
serpentine
serrated
serrogate   surrogate
serulean   cerulean
serum
servant
service
servicability
servile
sesame seed
sesarean   cesarean
sesquicentennial
sesquipedalian
session (meeting,
  see cession)
set-to
settee
settle

suer (one who sues, see sewer)		shamois	chamois
		shampoo	
		shamrock	
sevenfold		shamus	
seventeen		shananigans	shenanigans
seventy		shanghai	
sever (cut, see severe)		Shangri-La	
		shantecleer	chanticleer
several		shantung	
severance		shanty (cabin, see chantey)	
severe (serious, see sever)		sharecropper	
sewage		shartreuse	chartreuse
sewer (drain, see suer)		shatish	schottische
		shatter	
sew (mend, see so, sow)		shawl	
		sheaf	
sextet		shear (cut, see sheer)	
sexton			
sexual		sheath	
sfagnum	sphagnum	sheek	sheik (Arab leader) chic (stylish)
sfelte	svelte		
shabby			
shackle		sheef	sheaf
shaddock		sheen	
shadow		sheer (pure, see shear)	
shady			
shalac	shellac	sheik (Arab leader, see chic)	
shalacked	shellacked		
shale		shellac	
shalee	challis	shellacked	
shallot		shenanigans	
shallow		shenel	chenille
shaman		shenyon	chignon
shambles		shepherd	

sher	shirr	shrapnel	
sherbet		shred	
sheriff		shrew	
sherivere	charivari	shrewd	
sherry		shriek	
sheth	sheath	shrimp	
shevron	chevron	shrine	
shibboleth		shrink	
shicanery	chicanery	shrivel	
shifon	chiffon	shroud	
shifonier	chiffonier	shrub	
shield		shrubbery	
shillelagh		shuck	
shimmer		shudder	
shimmy		shuffle	
shingle		shun	
shirk		shuss	schuss
shirr		shutter	
shister	shyster	shuttlecock	
shivalry	chivalry	shyster	
shivere	charivari	sianamide	cyanamide
shiver		sianide	cyanide
shoal		siatic nerve	sciatic nerve
shoddy		sibilant	
shone (lighted,		sibling	
see shown)		sicamore	sycamore
shoot (discharge,		sicophant	sycophant
see chute)		sidereal	
shol	shoal	siege	
shorn		sierra	
shoulder		siesta	
shovel		sieve	
shower		sifless	syphilis
shown (displayed,		sifon	siphon
see shone)		sigh	

sight (see cite, site)		simultaneous	
sign		sinagogue	synagogue
signafy	signify	sincerely	
signal		sincerity	
signature		sinch	cinch
signet (seal, see cygnet)		sincopate	syncopate
		sindicate	syndicate
significant		sinecure	
signify		sinergism	synergism
silacate	silicate	sinester	sinister
silacon	silicon	sinew	
silage		singe	
silence		singleton	
silf	sylph	singular	
silhouette		sinister	
silicate		sink (submerge, see sync)	
silicon		sinnabar	cinnabar
sillogism	syllogism	sinner	
silo		sinod	synod
siloette	silhouette	sinopsis	synopsis
silvan	sylvan	sintax	syntax
simbiosis	symbiosis	sintillate	scintillate
simbiotic	symbiotic	sinuous	
simetar	scimitar	sinue	sinew
simian		sinus	
similar		sion	scion
simile		Sioux (Indians, see sou, sue)	
similitude			
simmer		siphon	
simplicity		sircum	succumb
simplification		siren	
simposium	symposium	siringa	syringa
simulate		siringe	syringe
simulcast		sirloin	

sisal		skittles	
sisegy	syzygy	skitzoid	schizoid
sissor	scissor	skitzophrenia	schizophrenia
sistern	cistern	sklerosis	sclerosis
sitadel	citadel	skulduggery	
sitar		skulk	
site (place, see cite, sight)		skull (head, see scull)	
sith	scythe	skullery	scullery
sitter		skullion	scullion
situate		skunk	
situation		slalom	
sitz bath		slander	
sive	sieve	slattern	
sivet	civet	slauch	slouch
sixpence		slaughter	
sixteenth		slavery	
sixth		slay (kill, see sleigh)	
sixty			
sizemograph	seismograph	sleazy	
sizzle		sledge	
skane	skein	sleek	
skeet		sleet	
skein		sleeve	
skeleton		sleezy	sleazy
skepernong	scuppernong	sleigh (sled, see slay)	
skerge	scourge		
skertzo	scherzo	sleight of hand (tricky, see slight)	
sketch			
skewer			
skimpy		slenderize	
skipper		sleuth	
skirmish		slew	
skism	schism	slight (frail, see sleight)	
skittish			

slight of hand	sleight of	smite
	hand	smithereens
slippage		smock
slippery		smolder
sloe (plum,		smooth
see slow)		smorgasbord
sloe-eyed		smother
sloe gin		smudge
slogan		smuggle
slolum	slalum	snafu
sloop		snail
slope		snapper
sloppy		sneakers
sloth		sneer
slouch		sneeze
slough		sniffle
slovenly		snippet
slow (not		snitch
quick, see sloe)		snivel
slow-eyed	sloe-eyed	snooze
slow gin	sloe gin	snorkel
sluce	sluice	snuggle
sludge		so (as a result,
slue	slew	see sew, sow)
sluggard		soar (fly high, see
sluggish		sore)
sluice		soared (flew, see
slurp		sword)
slur		sobriety
sluth	sleuth	sobriquet
smattering		soccer
smear		society
smelt		sociology
smirch		socket
smirk		sodality

sodden
sodemy   sodomy
soder   solder
sodium
sodium hydroxide
sodium nitrate
sodium pento-
    thal
sodomy
sofism   sophism
soggy
soilage
soiree
sojourn
solace
solar
solarium
solar plexus
solataire   solitaire
solatary   solitary
solder
soldier
sole (shoe,
    see soul)
solecism
soledarity   solidarity
solemn
solemnity
solicit
solicitude
solidarity
solidify
soliloquy
solitaire
solitary (alone,
    see salutary)

solstice
solubility
soluble
solution
solvent
somatic
sombrero
some (portion,
    see sum)
somersault
somnambulist
somniferous
son (male child,
    see sun)
sona   sauna
sonata
sonic
sonnet
sonorous
sonter   saunter
soothe
soothsayer
sooty
sophism
sophisticate
sophistry
sophomore
soporific
soprano
soral   sorrel
sorcery
sord   sword
sordid
sore (tender, see
    soar)
sorghum

soriasis	psoriasis	spasmodic	
sorority		spastic	
sorrel		spatial	
sorsery	sorcery	spatter	
sortie		spatula	
sot		spawn	
sou (French		speach	speech
coin, see Sioux,		speal	spiel
sue)		spearmint	
soubrette		specamen	specimen
souffle/soufflé		specie	
sought		specific	
soul (spirit, see		specify	
sole)		specimen	
soup		specious	
soupcon/soupçon		speckled	
source		spectacle	
sourkraut	sauerkraut	spectacular	
souse		spectator	
souvenir		specter	
sovereign		spectral	
sow (plant, see		spectroscope	
sew, so)		spectrum	
soybean		speculate	
spacial	spatial	speech	
spacious		speed	
spacific	specific	speedometer	
spaghetti		spelunk	
spangle		spermaceti	
spaniel		spermatocyte	
spanner		spesamen	specimen
sparkle		spew	
sparrow		sphagnum	
sparse		sphere	
spasm		sphincter	
spatchla	spatula	sphinx	

spicket   spigot   sprain
spicy   sprawl
spiel   spread
spigot   spright
spikelet   sprocket
spinach   spruce
spinal   spurious
spindle   sputnik
spinet   sputter
spinneret   squab
spinster   squabble
spiral   squadron
spiritual   squalid
  (religion)   squall
spirituel (re-   squalor
  fined)   squander
spiteful   squash
spittle   squat
spittoon   squaw
spleen   squawk
splendid   squeak
splendor   squeal
splice   squeamish
splinter   squeegee
sponge   squeeze
sponsor   squirm
spontaneity   squirrel
spontaneous   squirt
spoor (trail,   stability
  see spore)   staccato
sporadic   stadium
spore (seed, see   stagnant
  spoor)   stagnate
spouse

staid (dignified,
  see stayed)
stair (step, see
  stare)
stake (spike,
  see steak)
stalactite
stalagmite
stalemate
stallion
stalwart
stamen
stamina
stammer
stampede
stanchion
standard
stanza
staple
stare (look,
  see stair)
starve
static
stationary (fixed)
stationery
  (paper)
statistics
statue
stature
status
statute
statutory
stayed (remained,
  see staid)

steadfast
steady
steak (beef, see
  stake)
steal (purloin, see
  steel)
stealth
steam
steel (metal, see
  steal)
steep
steeple
steer
stein
stellar
stelth   stealth
stencil
stenographer
stenotype
stentorian
step (walk)
steppe (plain)
stereophonic
stereopticon
stereoscope
stereotype
sterile
sterling
stern
sternum
stethoscope
stevedore
steward

stich (line of
   verse, see stich)
stickler
stifle
stigma
stile (steps, see
   style)
stilted
stimie   stymie
stimulant
stimulate
stimulus
stipend
stipple
stiptic   styptic
stipulate
stirrup
stitch (sewing,
   see stich)
stockinet
stodgy
stogie
stoic
stolid
stolwort   stalwart
stomach
stooge
stoop (bend, see
   stoup, stupe)
stoup (large
   glass, see stoop,
   stupe)
stowaway
straddle

straight (direct,
   see strait)
strainer
strait (waterway,
   see straight)
strangle
strangulation
strategy
stratify
stratosphere
stratum
stratus
strawberry
streak
stream
strenuous
streptococcus
streptomycin
strewn
striate
stricken
stricknine   strychnine
stricture
strident
stringent
stroller
strontium
structure
strudel
struggle
strumpet
strychnine
stubborn
stucco

studious
stultify
stupe (medicated
  cloth, see
  stoop, stoup)
stupefy
stupendous
stupor
sturgeon
stutter
style (mode,
  see stile)
stylus
stymie
styptic
suacide   suicide
suade   suede
suave
subaltern
subret   soubrette
subconscious
subcontractor
suberb   suburb
subjugate
subjunctive
sublease
sublimate
sublime
subliminal
submarginal
submarine
submerge
submerse
submission

submit
subnormality
subordinate
suborn
subpoena
subscribe
subscription
subsedize   subsidize
subsedy   subsidy
subsequent
subservient
subsidiary
subsidize
subsidy
subsistence
subspecies
substance
substantial
substantiate
substantive
substitute
substratum
subterfuge
subterranean
subtle
subtropical
suburb
subversive
subvert
sucatash   succotash
succeed
success
succinct

suing		succor (relief, see	
suitable		sucker)	
suite (group,		succotash	
see sweet)		succulent	
succumb		suitor	
suceptible	susceptible	sulfa	
sucinct	succinct	sulfanilamide	
sucker (fish, see		sulfate	
succor)		sulfer	sulfur/sulphur
suction		sulfide	
sudden		sulfite	
sudo	pseudo	sulfur/sulphur	
sudonym	pseudonym	sullen	
sue (law, see		sulphur/sulfer	
Sioux, sou)		sultan	
suer (one who		sultry	
sues, see sewer)		sum (total, see	
suede		some)	
suet		sumac	
suffacate	suffocate	sumersault	somersault
suffer		summary (brief)	
sufferage	suffrage	summery (like	
sufferance		summer)	
suffice		summit	
sufficient		summon	
suffix		sumptuous	
suffle	souffle/	sun (star, see son)	
	soufflé	sundae (ice cream)	
suffocate		Sunday (Sabbath)	
suffrage		sunder	
suffuse		supena	subpoena
sufice	suffice	super	
suficient	sufficient	superabundance	
sugar		superannuate	
suggestible		superb	
suicide		supercilious	

superego		surf (waves,	
superficial		see serf)	
superfluous		surfeit	
superimpose		surge (wave,	
superintendent		see serge)	
superior		surgeon	
superlative		surgery	
supernumerary		surly	
supersaturate		surmise	
supersede		surmount	
supersession		surname	
supersonic		surpass	
superstition		surplice	
superstructure		surplus	
supervise		surprise	
supine		surrealism	
supper		surrender	
supplant		surreptitious	
supple		surrey	
supplement		surrogate	
suppliant		surround	
supplicate		surseas	surcease
supply		surveillance	
support		survey	
suppose		survive	
supposition		susceptible	
suppository		susinct	succinct
suppress		suspect	
supremacy		suspend	
supreme		suspender	
supress	suppress	suspension	
supson	soupcon/	suspicion	
	soupçon	sustaining	
surcease		sustenance	
surcharge		sutable	suitable
surely		sutle	subtle

suture		sycophant
suvenir	souvenir	sycosis (hair
svelte		disease, see
swabber		psychosis)
swagger		syllable
swain		syllabus
swallo (slug)		syllogism
swallow (bird)		sylph
swami		sylvan
swaree	soiree	symbiosis
swarthy		symbiotic
swashbuckler		symbol (sign, see
swastika		cymbal)
swatch		symbolism
swatter		symmetry
swave	suave	sympathy
swear		symphony
sweat		symposium
sweater		symptom
sweepstake		synagogue
sweet (sugar,		sync (abbr., syn-
see suite)		chronize, see
swelter		sink)
swerve		synchromesh
swimmer		synchronize
swindler		syncopate
swine		syndicate
swirl		syndrome
switch		synergism
swivel ·		synod
swizzle		synonym
swollen		synonymous
sword (weapon, see		synopsis
soared)		syntax
sycamore		synthesis

synthetic
syphen   siphon
sypher (joint,
   see cipher)
syphilis
syringa

syringe
syphless   syphilis
sysegy   syzygy
systalic
system
syzygy

T

tabacco	tobacco	taint	
tabasco		talc	
taber	tabor	talcum	
tabernacle		tale (story, see	
tableau		tail)	
tabloid		talisman	
tabogan	toboggan	talkative	
taboo		tallon	talon
tabor		tallow	
tabular		tallyho	
tabulate		Talmud	
tabulation		talo	tallow
tabulator		talon	
tacit		tamarack	
taciturn		tambourine	
tackle		tandamount	tantamount
tact		tandem	
tactics		tangel	tangle
tactile		tangent	
taffeta		tangential	
tail (end, see		tangerine	
tale)		tangible	
tailor (clothes		tangle	
maker, see		tankard	
Taylor)		tannery	

tantalize		taupe (color, see	
tantamount		tope)	
tantrum		taut (stretched,	
taper (narrow,		see taught)	
see tapir)		tautology	
tapestry		tavern	
tapioca		tawdry	
tapir (animal,		taxi	
see taper)		taxidermist	
tapistry	tapestry	Taylor (name, see	
tappioca	tapioca	tailor)	
tarantula		tea (drink, see	
tardy		tee)	
tare (weed, see		teakwood	
tear)		team (squad, see	
taregon	tarragon	teem)	
target		tear (rip, see tare)	
tariff		tear (cry, see tier)	
tarnish		teara	tiara
tarpaulin		tease	
tarpon		teat	
tarragon		teathe	teethe
tarriff	tariff	teatmouse	titmouse
tarry		teatotaler	teetotaler
tartar		tebercular	tubercular
tartare sauce		teberculosis	tuberculosis
tasit	tacit	technical	
tasiturn	taciturn	technician	
tassel		Technicolor	
tattered		technique	
tattle		technology	
tattoo		tedious	
taught (did		tedium	
teach, see taut)		tee (peg, see tea)	
taunt		teekwood	teakwood

teem (swarm, see
    team)
teeth (pl. tooth)
teethe (cut teeth)
teetotaler
telecast
telegraph
teleology
telepathy
telescope
telescopic
teletype
temerity
temper
tempera (painting
    medium, see
    tempura)
temperament
temperance
temperate
temperature
temperize   temporize
temperment   temperament
tempest
tempestuous
tempis fugit   tempus fugit
template
temple
temporal
temporarily
temporary
temporize
tempt
temptable
temptation

tempura (Japan-
    ese dish, see
    tempera)
tempus fugit
tenable
tenacious
tenacity
tenacle   tentacle
tenament   tenement
tenant
tendency
tendentious
tender
tenderloin
tendon
tendril
Tenebrae
tenement
tenible   tenable
tennable   tenable
tennacious   tenacious
tennant   tenant
tennis
tenor
tense
tensile strength
tension
tensor
tantacle
tentative
tenterhooks
tenuous
tenure
tepee
tepid

tequila		testament	
terantula	tarantula	testicle	
terban	turban	testify	
terbine	turbine	testimonial	
terbulent	turbulent	testimony	
tereen	tureen	testosterone	
terific	terrific	tetanus	
termagant		tete-a-tete/tête-á-tête	
terminable		tether	
terminal		tetrachloride	
terminate		tetrahedron	
terminology		tetralogy	
terminus		tetrameter	
termite		tetrarch	
termoil	turmoil	Teutonic	
tern (bird, see		textile	
turn)		textual	
terodactyl	pterodactyl	textural	
terquoise	turquoise	texture	
terrace		thalamus	
terra cotta		thalidomide	
terrain		than (comparative,	
terramycin		see then)	
terrapin		thatched	
terrazzo		thealogian	theologian
terrestrial		thearetical	theoretical
terrible		theater/theatre	
terrier		theif	thief
terrific		their (poss. see	
terrify		there, they're)	
territorial		theism	
territory		theistic	
terror		theive	thieve
terse		thematic	
tertiary		theme	

then (at another time, see than)		thirsty	
thence		thirteen	
theocracy		thirtieth	
theologian		thirty	
theology		thistle	
theorem		thither	
theoretical		thoracic	
theorist		thorax	
theorize		thorobred	thoroughbred
theory		thorough (com-plete, see through)	
theosophy			
therapeutic		thoroughbred	
therapy		though	
there (place, see their, they're)		thought	
		thousand	
		threadbare	
thermal		threaten	
thermodynamics		thresher	
thermometer		threshold	
thermonuclear		thrice	
thermos		throat	
thermostat		throes (pain, see throws)	
therum	theorem		
thesaurus		thrombosis	
thesis		throttle	
thesorus	thesaurus	through (pene-trate, see thor-ough)	
Thespian			
they're (they are, see their, there)		throws (does throw, see throes)	
thiamine			
thicket		thug	
thief		thumb	
thieve		thunderous	
thigh			
thimus	thymus	thursty	thirsty

thwart		tinsel	
thyme (herb, see		tintinnabulation	
time)		tiny	
thymus		tiphoid	typhoid
thyroid		tiphoon	typhoon
tiara		tipify	typify
tic (twitch)		tirade	
tick (sound)		tirannical	tyrannical
ticket		tire	
tickle		tiro/tyro	
ticktacktoe		tissue	
ticoon	tycoon	tit	teat
tidal		titel	title
tiddlywinks		tithe	
tier (row, see		titian	
tear)		titillate	
tigress		title	
tike	tyke	titmouse	
tile		titular	
timbal (drum)		to (preposition,	
timbale (food)		see too, two)	
timber (wood)		toad	
timbre (sound)		toastmaster	
time (minute,		tobacco	
see thyme)		toboggan	
timidity		tocsin (signal,	
timorous		see toxin)	
timpani (drum,		tode	toad
see tympany)		toddy	
timpany	tympany	toe (foot digit,	
tin		see tow)	
tincel	tinsel	toehead	towhead
tincture		toga	
tine		together	
tinge		toggle	
tingle			

tole (painted tin, see toll)		topic	
tolerable		topple	
tolerant		topsy-turvy	
tolerate		Torah	
toll (tax, see tole)		torchous	tortuous
		toreador	
tollerable	tolerable	torent	torrent
tomahawk		torential	torrential
tomaine	ptomaine	torid	torrid
tomato		torment	
tomb		tornado	
tomfoolery		tornament	tournament
tommahawk	tomahawk	torpedo	
tomorrow		torpid	
tonage	tonnage	torpor	
tonal		torque	
toncil	tonsil	Torrah	Torah
toncillectomy	tonsillec-tomy	torreador	toreador
		torrent	
toncillitis	tonsillitis	torrential	
tongue		torrid	
tonic		torsion	
tonight		torso	
tonnage		tort (civil wrong)	
tonsil		torte (dessert)	
tonsillectomy		tortilla	
tonsillitis		tortoise	
tonsorial		tortuous	
too (also, see to, two)		torture	
		total	
tooth		totalitarian	
toothache		totality	
topaz		totem	
tope (to drink, see taupe)		touch	
		touche/touché	

tough		trajectory	
tought	taught	trammeled	
toupee		trample	
tour de force		trampoline	
tourist		trance	
tournament		tranquil	
tourney		tranquilizer	
tourniquet		transact	
toushe	touche/	transatlantic/	
	touché	trans-Atlantic	
tow (cart, see		transcend	
toe)		transcendental	
toward		transcribe	
towel		transcription	
tower		transe	trance
towhead		transend	transcend
town		transendental	transcendental
toxic		transfer	
toxin (poison,		transference	
see tocsin)		transfiguration	
trace		transfixed	
trachea		transformation	
trachoma		transfusion	
tractable		transgress	
traction		transience	
tractor		transient	
tradition		transistor	
traffic		transition	
trafficker		transitional	
tragectory	trajectory	transitive	
tragedy		transitory	
tragic		translate	
trailer		translucent	
train		transmigration	
trait		transmit	
traitor		transmittal	

transmitter		treat	
transmute		treatise	
transom		treaty	
transparent		treble	
transpire		tred	tread
transplant		trefoil	
transport		trek	
transpose		trekked	
transposition		trellis	
transverse		tremble	
transvestite		tremendous	
tranzlucent	translucent	tremolo	
trapeze		tremor	
trapezoid		tremulous	
trapper		trenchant	
Trappist		trepidation	
trase	trace	trespasser	
trate	trait	tressel	trestle
trauma		trestle	
traumatic		trial	
travail		triangle	
travel		tribal	
travelogue		tribe	
traverse		tribulation	
travesty		tribune	
trawler		tributary	
treacherous		tribute	
treachery		triceps	
treacle		trichina	
treacly		trichinosis	
treadle		trickery	
treadmill		trickle	
treason		tricycle	
treasure		trident	
treasurer		triennial	

trifling		trotter	
trigger		troubadour	
trilingual		trouble	
trillion		trough	
trillium		troul	trowel
trilogy		troupe (per-	
trimming		formers, see	
trinity		troop)	
trinket		trousers	
trio		trousseau	
tripartite		trout	
triple		trowel	
triplet		truancy	
triptych		truant	
triumph		trubadour	troubadour
triumvirate		truce	
trivet		truckage	
trivia		truculence	
trivial		trudge	
troche (lozenge)		true	
trochee (meter)		truency	truancy
trodden		truent	truant
troff	trough	truffle	
troglodyte		trumpeter	
trojectory	trajectory	truncate	
trolley		trundle bed	
trollop		truso	trousseau
trombone		truss	
troop (soldiers,		trustee (adminis-	
see troupe)		trator, see	
tropesphere	troposphere	trusty)	
trophy		trustful	
tropic		trustworthy	
tropism		trusty (reliable,	
troposphere		see trustee)	

trysting
tsar/czar
tsetse fly
tubercular
tuberculosis
tuberous
tubular
tufted
tuition
tularemia
tumoltuous   tumultuous
tumor
tumultuous
tundra
tungsten
tunic
tunnel
tupee   toupee
turban
turbine
turbulent
tureen
turgid
turmoil
turn (rotate,
  see tern)
turnament   tournament
turney   tourney
turnip   tourniquet
turniquet
turnstile
turpentine
turpitude
turquoise
turret

tushe   touche/touché
tussle
tutelage
tutelary
Tutonic   Teutonic
tutor
toxedo
twain
tweak
tweed
tweeter
tweezer
twelfth
twentieth
twenty
tweter   tweeter
twezer   tweezer
twich   twitch
twilight
twinge
twinkle
twirl
twitch
two (number,
  see to, too)
tycoon
tyfoid   typhoid
tyfoon   typhoon
tyfus   typhus
tyke
tympany (bom-
  bast, see
  timpani)
typeographical   typograph-
                    ical

typewriter
typhoid
typhoon
typhus
typical
typify

typographical
typography
tyrannical
tyranny
tyrant
tyro/tiro

U

ubiquitous
ucalyptus — eucalyptus
Ucharist — Eucharist
uchre — euchre
udder (gland,
  see utter)
udomoter
ufemism — euphemism
ufonic — euphonic
ugenic — eugenic
ugh
ukulele
ulcer
ulceration
ulcerous
ulogistic — eulogistic
ulogize — eulogize
ulogy — eulogy
ultamatum — ultimatum
ulterior
ultimate
ultimatum
ultraviolet
umber
umbilical cord

umbrage
umbrella
umlaut
umph — oomph
unabridged
unaccountable
unaccustomer
unaffected
unanimity
unanimous
unassuming
unavoidable
unbeknownst
unbiased
unbidden
unbridled
uncanny
unceremonious
uncertainty
uncivilized
uncle
uncomfortable
uncommitted
uncommon
uncommunicative

uncompromising	unharnessed
unconditional	unhurried
unconscionable	unicameral
unconscious	unicorn
unconstitutional	unification
uncouth	uniformity
unction	unify
unctuous	unilateral
undaunted	unimpeachable
undemonstrative	unique
undeniable	unison
undercurrent	unitary
undernourished	universal
undesirable	universe
undoubtedly	university
undulation	unkempt
unduly	unknowable
uneasiness	unleash
unemployable	unlimited
unequal	unmentionable
unequivocal	unmercifully
unerring	unmitigated
unexpurgated	unnatural
unfamiliarity	unnecessary
unfaned unfeigned	unnumbered
unfasten	unoccupied
unfeigned	unparalleled
unfettered	unplumbed
unflinching	unprecedented
unforgettable	unprejudiced
unfortunate	unprincipled
unfriendliness	unpronounceable
unfurled	unqualified
ungainliness	unquestionable
ungrateful	unraveled
unhappiness	unreality

unremitting	uphoria	euphoria
unrighteous	upward	
unrivaled	uranium	
unruffled	urban	
unsaturated	urbane	
unsavory	urchin	
unseasonable	ureka	eureka
unseemly	urethra	
unshackled	urgent	
unsheathe	urinal	
unsophisticated	urinary	
unsparing	urn	
unsuitable	urology	
untangled	usher	
untrammeled	ustachian tube	Eustachian tube
untutored	usurp	
unuch eunuch	usury	
unusual	utensil	
unwanted	uterine	
unwarrantable	uterus	
unwary	uthanasia	euthanasia
unwholesome	utilitarian	
unwieldy	utility	
unwitting	utopian	
unwonted	utter (speak, see	
upheaval	udder)	
uphemism euphuism	utterance	
upholstery	uvula	
uphonic euphonic		

V

vabrato	vibrato	valence (weights, see valance)	
vacant		valentine	
vacation		valese	valise
vaccinate		valet	
vaccine		valiant	
vaccum	vacuum	valid	
vacillate		validity	
vacsinate	vaccinate	valise	
vacsine	vaccine	valley	
vacuity		valocity	velocity
vacuous		valor	
vacuum		valour	velour
vagabond		valuable	
vagary		valuminous	voluminous
vagina		valuptuous	voluptuous
vagrancy		vampire	
vague		vanacular	vernacular
vain (idle, see vane, vein)		vandal	
vainglorious		vane (weather-cock, see vain, vein)	
valance (drapery, see valence)			
vale (valley, see veil)		vaneer	veneer
valedictorian		vanguard	
		vanilla	

vanity	vellum	
vanquish	velocity	
vantage	velour	
vapid	velvet	
vapor	venal	
vaporous	venason	venison
variant	vender/vendor	
varicose vein	vendetta	
variegate	veneal	veniel
variety	veneer	
various	venerable	
varsity	venerate	
vary (change,	venereal	
see very)	vengeance	
vascular	vengeful	
vas deferens	venial	
vasectomy	venison	
vasomotor	venom	
vassal	venomous	
vassalage	venous	
vaudeville	ventilate	
vault	ventilator	
veal	ventral	
vecissitude visissitude	ventriloquist	
vector	venture	
veer	venue	
vegetable	venum	venom
vegetarian	venus	venous
vegetate	veola	viola
vehement	veracious (truth,	
vehicle	see voracious)	
veil (screen, see	veracose vein	varicose vein
vale)	veranda	
vein (channel, see	verbal	
vain, vane)	verbatim	

verbena		vestal	
verbiage		vestibule	
verbose		vestige	
verboten		vestigial	
verdant		vetch	
verdict		veteran	
verdure		veterinary	
verge		vexation	
verify		vi	vie
verily		via	
verisimilitude		viable	
veritable		viaduct	
verity		vial (cup, see	
vermicelli		vile)	
vermilion		vialable	violable
vermin		viand	
vermouth		vibrate	
vernacular		vibrato	
vernal equinox		vibrator	
verranda	veranda	vicar	
versatile		vicarious	
verse		vice (defect, see	
versification		vise)	
version		vice versa	
versus		vichyssoise	
vertebra		vicinity	
vertebrate		vicious	
vertex		vicissitude	
vertical		victim	
vertigo		victor	
very (much,		victual	
see vary)		vicuna/vicuña	
vesheswase	vichyssoise	video	
vespers		vie	
vessel		viend	viand

vigil
vigilance
vigilante
vignette
vigor
viament   vehement
vile (foul, see
    vial)
vilify
village
villain (rogue)
villein (serf)
vinaigrette sauce
vinal   vinyl
vincible
vindetta   vendetta
vindicate
vindictive
vinegar
vinegret sauce   vinaigrette
                 sauce
vineyard
vintage
vinyet   vignette
vinyl
viola
violable
violate
violence
violet
violin
viper
virago
virgin
virile

virtual
virtue
virtuosity
virtuoso
virtuous
virulence
virus
visa
visage
vis-a-vis/vis-à-vis
visceral
viscose
viscount
vise (tool, see
    vice)
viseral   visceral
visheswase   vichyssoise
visible
vision
visitor
visor
vissage   visage
vista
visual
vitality
vitamin
vitiate
vitrefy   vitrify
vitreous
vitrify
vitriol
vittal   victual
vituperate
vivacious
vivacity

vivesection	vivisection	voluminous
vivid		voluntary
viviparous		volunteer
vivisection		voluptuous
vizier		voodoo
vizor	visor	voracious (engulf-
vocabulary		ing, see veracious)
vocalize		voracity
vociferous		vortex
vodka		vortical
vodville	vaudeville	votary
vogue		voucher
voice		vowel
voile		voyage
volatile		voyeur
volcano		vulcanize
volition		vulgar
Volkswagen		Vulgate
volley		vulnerable
volocity	velocity	vulture
voltage		vulva
voluble		vying
volume		

W

waddle

wafe   waif

wafer

waffle

waft

wager

waggish

wagon

waif

wail (cry, see
    wale, whale)

wain (cart, see
    wane)

wainscot

waist (between
    chest and hips,
    see waste)

wait (postpone,
    see weight)

waive (forgo, see
    wave)

walaby   wallaby

wale (texture,
    see wail, whale)

walet   wallet

walkie-talkie

wallaby

wallet

walleyed pike

wallop

wallow

walnut

walrus

waltz

wammy   whammy

wampum

wanderer

wane (decrease,
    see wain)

wangle

wanton

warbler

warden

wardrobe

ware (articles,
    see wear, where)

warehouse

warf   wharf

warn

warrant

warranty
warrior
wary
wash
wassail
Wassermann test
waste (squander,
  see waist)
wastrel
watt (electric,
  see what)
wattle
wavering
wave (fluctuate,
  see waive)
waxen
way (route, see
  weigh, whey)
we (all of us, see
  oui)
weak (feeble, see
  week)
weal (welt, see
  we'll, wheal,
  wheel)
wealth
wean
weapon
wear (put on, see
  ware, where)
wearisome
wearwolf   werewolf
weary
weasel
weather (climate,
  see whether,
  wether)

weave
                   weevil
webbing
wedding
wedge
Wedgie
Wedgwood ware
wedlock
wee   we (all of us)
                  oui (yes)
weedle   wheedle
weege board ouija board
week (time, see
  weak)
ween   wean
weesel   weasel
weeve   weave
weevil
weigh (measure,
  see way, whey)
weight (measure,
  see wait)
weird
weld
welfare
we'll (we will, see
  wheal, weal,
  wheel)
welterweight
wence   whence
werewolf
wery   wary
westerner
westward
wether (ram, see
  weather, whether)
wetstone   whetstone

whale (mammal,
  see wail, wale)
whammy
wharf
what (pronoun,
  see watt)
wheal (welt, see
  weal, we'll,
  wheel)
wheat
wheedle
wheel (tire, see
  weal, we'll,
  wheal)
wheeze
whence
where (place,
  see ware, wear)
wherry
whether (con-
  junction, see
  weather,
  wether)
whetstone
whey (curds and,
  see way, weigh)
which (pronoun,
  see wich, witch)
whiff
Whig (political
  party, see wig)
while (conjunction,
  see wile)
whimper
whimple   wimple
whimsey

whimsical
whine (cry, see
  wine)
whinny
whiporwill   whippoorwill
whippersnapper
whippet
whippoorwill
whirl
whisk broom
whiskey/whisky
whisper
whist
whistle
whither (where
  to, see wither)
whittle
whiz
whoa
whole (all, see
  hole)
whoopee
whooping cough
whopper
whore (prostitute,
  see hoar)
whorl
who's (who is)
whose (possessive)
wich (tree, see
  which, witch)
wicked
wicker
wicket
widow
width

wield		witch (woman,		
wiff	whiff	see which,		
wig (hair, see		wich)		
Whig)		witicism	witticism	
wiggle		wither (shrivel,		
wigwam		see whither)		
wilderness		witness		
wile (trick,		witticism		
see while)		wizard		
will-o'-the-wisp		wizen		
willow		wobble		
willy-nilly		woebegone		
wimple		woeful		
wimper	whimper	woffer	woofer	
wimsey	whimsey	wolverine		
wimsical	whimsical	womb		
wince		wombat		
winch		wonder		
window		wondrous		
wine (drink,		wont (habit)		
see whine)		won't (will not)		
winnow		woo		
winsome		wood (lumber,		
wiper		see would)		
wippersnapper	whipper-	woofer		
	snapper	wooppee	whooppee	
wipporwill	whippoorwill	Worcestershire		
wisdom		sauce		
wiseacre		world		
wiskbroom	whiskbroom	worse		
wist	whist	worship		
wistaria/wisteria		worst (bad, see		
Wistershire sauce	Worcestershire	wurst)		
	sauce	worsted		

Worstershire   Worcester-   wrestler
  sauce   shire sauce   wretch (vile
would (past   person, see
  tense of will,   retch)
  see wood)   wriggle
wound   wright (play-
wraith   wright, see right,
wrangler   rite, write)
wrapped (cover,   wrinkle
  see rapped,   wrist
  rapt)   writ
wrath   write (jot down,
wreak (inflict,   see right, rite,
  see reek)   wright)
wreath   writhe
wreathe   wrong
wreck   wrought
wren   wry (bent, see
wrench   rye)
wrest (distort,   wurst (meat,
  see rest)   see worst)

X

xenophobia
Xerox
X-ray

xylocaine
xylophone

Y

yacht
yak
yawn
yearning
yeast
yellow
yeoman
yesterday
Yiddish
yield
yodel
yogurt/yoghurt

yogi
yoke (frame,
  see yolk)
yolk (egg, see
  yoke)
yoman   yeoman
Yom Kuppur
your (possessive)
you're (you are)
yowl
yuletide

Z

zeal   zither
zealot   zodiac
zealous   zombi
zelot   zealot   zone
zenith   zoological
zennia   zinnia   zoology
zenophobia   xenophobia Zoroastrian
zephyr   zucchini
zeppelin   zwieback
zero   zygote
zinc   zylocaines   xylocaines
zinnia   zylophone   xylophone
zipper